TAKE ALL YOUR CHANCES

AT BRIDGE

Eddie Kantar

Master Point Press
331 Douglas Ave.
Toronto, Ontario, Canada
M5M 1H2 (416)781-0351

Email: info@masterpointpress.com

Websites: www.masterpointpress.com
www.masteringbridge.com
www.bridgeblogging.com
www.ebooksbridge.com

Library and Archives Canada Cataloguing in Publication

Kantar, Edwin B., 1932-
Take all your chances (at bridge) / Eddie Kantar.

ISBN 978-1-897106-55-6

1. Contract bridge. I. Title.

GV1282.435.K357 2009 795.41'53 C2009-904838-8

Editor Ray Lee
Copy editor/interior format Sally Sparrow
Cover and interior design Olena S. Sullivan/New Mediatrix

1 2 3 4 5 6 7 13 12 11 10 09

PRINTED IN CANADA

TABLE OF CONTENTS

INTRODUCTION

On many bridge hands you can see more than one reasonable line of play to make your contract. If you select the best percentage line your chance of making the hand increases, but if you don't... There's a better way to go, though. The idea is to look for the line of play which, if it doesn't work, still allows you to try the other line; there may even be a third line! This is called 'staying alive', a phrase which could just as well be the title of this book. In other words, avoid putting all of your eggs in one basket!

Unfortunately, but realistically, there will be hands where you have to choose immediately among several lines of play. The opponents have forced your hand and there is no time to try one line and then switch to another if the first doesn't work. Now it does help to know a bit about percentages or the odds. Some of these percentages, *common* ones, will be sprinkled throughout the book. You are probably familiar with most of them already, but if you are not, these numbers can help. A list of the most helpful percentage numbers can be found at the end of the book (Appendix 2, p.165).

How should you attack the hands where you do have options available? If you are declaring a notrump contract, count your sure tricks. If you don't have enough to make the contract (and you won't!) look for some way to develop that missing trick or tricks. If you see at least two lines of play to secure those extra tricks, look for a way to stay alive! Give yourself a chance to take both lines. At trump contracts counting losers *and* sure tricks is the way to go. If the total doesn't come to thirteen, count your cards.

Many common themes have been introduced with a few purposeful 'theme repeats'. The repeats give you a chance to see if you picked up some pointers from a somewhat similar previous example. Some of these hands are from articles and books I have written, others I have constructed especially for this book.

The East-West hands listed at the end of the commentary are arbitrary. They are set up for teachers so that the student (and/or you) will at least be rewarded for selecting the best percentage line. In real life, unfortunately, the best percentage line is not always the winning line.

The bidding will be given and explained with only a rare exception (you, or more likely partner, having made a bid that defies explanation). Use the bidding where you can as a guide in the play.

Assume IMP scoring. *Play to make your contract and do not worry about overtricks or undertricks.* If the play would differ at matchpoints, it will be mentioned in the discussion.

After the bidding and the opening lead (assume fourth best leads) you will eventually see 'Plan the play' and that is your cue to stop reading and start planning before reading on. Four play problems are followed by their solutions on the following pages. Restrain yourself — try to solve each problem yourself rather than just turning the page!

The difficulty level is intermediate to intermediate plus. The more difficult hands are labeled 'advanced' so take double credit for those. Have fun! Onward!

Eddie Kantar

THE PROBLEMS

PROBLEM 1

♠ K 8 4 2
♡ K 7 5
♢ A Q J 10 2
♣ A

♠ 3
♡ A Q J 10 9 6 4 3
♢ 9 8
♣ 10 4

After you open 4♡, partner checks to make sure you have an ace and sets you down in 6♡. Opening lead: ♣K. Plan the play.

PROBLEM 2 (*ADVANCED*)

♠ Q J
♡ 7
♢ 7 5 4 2
♣ A K 7 5 4 2

♠ A 7 6
♡ A 10 8 5 2
♢ A K 3
♣ Q 6

You open 1♡, partner responds 2♣ (intending to rebid 3♣, invitational), but your jump to 3NT ends the bidding. If a 2♣ response is played as a game force, then 1NT (forcing) is the proper response. You would raise 1NT to 2NT and partner would bid 3NT. All roads lead to Rome.

The opening lead is the ♠4 and dummy's ♠J wins, East playing the ♠3, showing count. Plan the play.

PROBLEM 3

♠ A Q 4
♡ A Q
♢ J 9 8 3 2
♣ 7 3 2

♠ K 8
♡ 5 4 2
♢ A 6 4
♣ A Q J 10 4

You decide to treat your hand as worth 15 points (look at those clubs) and open 1NT. Partner raises you to 3NT and you wind up playing the hand from the wrong side. Let's hope partner doesn't count your points. West leads the ♡J. You try the ♡Q, but no luck: East wins and returns the ♡8 to dummy's ♡A. When you lead a club to the ♣Q, it holds. Plan the play from here.

PROBLEM 4 (*ADVANCED*)

♠ A 7 5
♡ J 10 9
♢ K 8 6 4 2
♣ 9 4

♠ K 8 4 2
♡ A Q
♢ A 5 3
♣ A K 8 6

The auction 2NT-3NT gets you the opening lead of the ♡4, East playing the ♡2 (standard count). And now? Plan the play.

SOLUTION 1

♠ K 8 4 2
♡ K 7 5
◇ A Q J 10 2
♣ A

♠ 3
♡ A Q J 10 9 6 4 3
◇ 9 8
♣ 10 4

After you open 4♡, partner checks to make sure you have an ace and sets you down in 6♡. Opening lead: ♣K. Plan the play.

You have two possible losers, a spade and a diamond, and you have two chances to get rid of at least one of them.

You can take the diamond finesse. If it wins, you make an overtrick, if it loses you are down one as the ♠A is the setting trick. Alternatively, you can lead up to the ♠K first. If West has the ♠A, you won't need the diamond finesse as a diamond goes off on the ♠K assuming West goes up with the ♠A. If West plays low, the ♠K wins and you can take the diamond finesse for an overtrick. If East tops the ♠K with the ♠A, you still have the diamond finesse available.

Tip

When two lines of play are available, take the one that gives you a chance (keeps you alive) to use the other if the first fails. Expect this theme ('staying alive') to appear time and again in this set of hands, just as at the table. Lead up to the ♠K to stay alive.

Percentage-wise if you lead up to the ♠K first and that doesn't work and then take the diamond finesse you have a 75% chance of making the hand. (One of two finesses.)

If you put all of your eggs in the diamond finesse basket you only have a 50% chance of making the hand.

The West hand: ♠A 9 6 5 ♡2 ◇7 6 4 3 ♣K Q J 9
The East hand: ♠Q J 10 7 ♡8 ◇K 5 ♣8 7 6 5 3 2

SOLUTION 2 (*ADVANCED*)

♠ Q J
♡ 7
◇ 7 5 4 2
♣ A K 7 5 4 2

♠ A 7 6
♡ A 10 8 5 2
◇ A K 3
♣ Q 6

You open 1♡, partner responds 2♣ (intending to rebid 3♣, invitational), but your jump to 3NT ends the bidding. If a 2♣ response is played as a game force, then 1NT (forcing) is the proper response. You would raise 1NT to 2NT and partner would bid 3NT. All roads lead to Rome.

The opening lead is the ♠4 and dummy's ♠J wins, East playing the ♠3, count. Plan the play.

You have eight top tricks and need but one more. In spite of those impressive clubs, if you rely entirely on a 3-2 break, you will be giving yourself a 68% chance to make the hand. Not bad, but you can do better. Much better. Duck a diamond at Trick 2, win the likely spade return and play the ◇A and ◇K. If diamonds break 3-3 (36%), dummy's fourth diamond is your ninth trick. If they don't, you still have 3-2 clubs to fall back on (68%). You stay alive by playing diamonds before clubs, giving yourself an 80% chance of making the hand. Why consign the diamonds to oblivion? It doesn't cost anything to test them. Take full credit if you played the ◇A, ◇K and another diamond instead of ducking a diamond.

Notice that you can't test the clubs first and fall back on the diamonds being 3-3 if the clubs don't break 3-2. The club suit is the entry to the fourth diamond; diamonds have to be attacked before clubs.

The West hand: ♠K 10 8 4 2 ♡Q 9 4 3 ◇J 9 8 ♣9
The East hand: ♠9 5 3 ♡K J 6 ◇Q 10 6 ♣J 10 8 3

SOLUTION 3

♠ A Q 4
♡ A Q
◊ J 9 8 3 2
♣ 7 3 2

♠ K 8
♡ 5 4 2
◊ A 6 4
♣ A Q J 10 4

You decide to treat your hand as worth 15 points (look at those clubs) and open 1NT. Partner raises you to 3NT and you wind up playing the hand from the wrong side. Let's hope partner doesn't count your points. West leads the ♡J. You try the ♡Q, but no luck: East wins and returns the ♡8 to dummy's ♡A. When you lead a club to the ♣Q, it holds. Plan the play from here.

You need five club tricks to make the contract and it looks like East has the needed ♣K. One possibility is to cash three spades discarding a diamond and repeat the club finesse. If East has ♣Kx or ♣Kxx you score five club tricks, or ten tricks in all.

But what if East has four clubs headed by the ♣K? In that case you will need *two additional* dummy entries to take two more club finesses. The safe way to take five club tricks is to *overtake* the ♠K, take a second club finesse, and assuming West shows out, cross to the ♠Q and take a third club finesse. You wind up with nine tricks (and a grateful partner). Five clubs, two spades and two red aces.

This hand is one of many that illustrate the difference between the strategy for playing a hand at IMPs and at matchpoints. At IMPs you don't worry that much about overtricks because your primary concern is making your contract with minimum risk. At matchpoints, however, you often risk the contract for the sake of an overtrick (or two) providing the odds favor the risk. On this hand the odds favor the risk. It is far more likely that East has two or three clubs headed by the king than four clubs headed by the king. At matchpoints, cash three spades and repeat the club finesse one last time.

The West hand: ♠ J 6 5 3 2 ♡ J 10 9 7 3 ◊ Q 5 ♣ 6
The East hand: ♠ 10 9 7 ♡ K 8 6 ◊ K 10 7 ♣ K 9 8 5

SOLUTION 4 (*ADVANCED*)

♠ A 7 5
♡ J 10 9
♢ K 8 6 4 2
♣ 9 4

♠ K 8 4 2
♡ A Q
♢ A 5 3
♣ A K 8 6

The auction 2NT-3NT gets you the opening lead of the ♡4, East playing the ♡2 (standard count). And now? Plan the play.

It looks very much as if hearts are 5-3 which means you must score nine tricks before they can get in twice. The good news is that you start with eight sure tricks. This should be your plan:

Play the ♢A and ♢K; if both follow, give up a diamond ensuring ten tricks. If diamonds are 4-1, duck a spade. You still make 3NT if spades are 3-3.

If you duck a diamond early and diamonds are 4-1, down you go. They play a second heart and now you don't have time to set up a ninth trick in spades if the suit is divided 3-3. It is crucial to see how diamonds break *before* conceding a diamond trick. There are two suits involved here, not just one.

The West hand: ♠J 9 3 ♡K 8 7 4 3 ♢Q 10 9 7 ♣J
The East hand: ♠Q 10 6 ♡6 5 2 ♢J ♣Q 10 7 5 3 2

PROBLEM 5 (*ADVANCED*)

♠ A 10
♡ 9 4 3 2
◇ K Q 6 5
♣ J 7 3

♠ K Q 6 4
♡ A K J
◇ A J 10 9 8 7
♣ —

A jump shift followed by a jump preference from partner (1◇-1♡; 2♠-4◇), then control bids of 4♡ from you and 4♠ from partner, lands you in a touchy grand slam. Your contract is 7◇ and the opening lead is the ♣K. Plan your Grand Slam play.

PROBLEM 6

♠ A J 4
♡ J 10
◇ A K J 10
♣ Q 10 9 8

♠ K 10 3 2
♡ K Q
◇ 6 5
♣ A K J 7 6

After you open 1♣ and bid 1♠ over partner's 1◇ response, partner invites slam in clubs, starting with a fourth suit 2♡ bid, and then supporting clubs after you leap to 3NT. You check for keycards and after finding two aces you trot out 6♣, the final contract. The opening lead is the ♡9. East wins the ♡A and returns a heart. Clubs are 2-2. Plan the play.

PROBLEM 7

♠ K J 10
♡ 10 4 2
◇ J 5 3
♣ A Q J 5

♠ A Q 9 8 4 3
♡ A K J 5
◇ Q 8 2
♣ —

With both sides vulnerable, West opens 1◇, North and East pass, you double, partner responds 3♣ (being too strong to make a forced 2♣ response). You bid 3♠, forcing, and partner raises to 4♠. Incidentally, when either making or responding to a takeout double, devalue jacks and queens in any suit or suits the opponents have bid unless you (1) are responding in notrump; (2) have a death wish.

West leads the ◇A, ◇K and another diamond. East trumps the third diamond and exits with a low heart. Spades are 2-2. What is your plan? (Notice that the ◇J and ◇Q were worthless.)

PROBLEM 8 (*ADVANCED*)

♠ 4 3
♡ K J 8 6 5
◇ A 9 6
♣ A 5 4

♠ A Q
♡ A Q 10 9 4 3
◇ K 5 4 2
♣ 7

After you open 1♡ and partner responds 2NT, Jacoby, you show your singleton club and partner bids 3◇. You bid 4NT, Keycard Blackwood, and land in 6♡. The opening lead is the ♣Q. Hearts are 1-1. Plan the play.

SOLUTION 5 (*ADVANCED*)

♠ A 10
♡ 9 4 3 2
◇ K Q 6 5
♣ J 7 3

♠ K Q 6 4
♡ A K J
◇ A J 10 9 8 7
♣ —

A jump shift followed by a jump preference from partner (1◇-1♡; 2♠-4◇), then control bids of 4♡ from you and 4♠ from partner, lands you in a touchy grand slam. Your contract is 7◇ and the opening lead is the ♣K. Plan your Grand Slam play.

You have a possible heart loser, a loser that can be avoided if East has the ♡Q. On the other hand, if West has the ♠J, you can lead a spade to the ♠10. If the ♠10 holds you can discard two hearts from dummy on the ♠KQ. No more heart loser. In other words, you are looking at two finesses and if either works you can make your grand slam — but if you take the wrong one… down you go. If only you knew which one to take.

Tip

When either of two finesses will give you your contract, one suit missing a queen, the other a jack, play the ace and king of the suit missing the queen (here, hearts). If the queen doesn't appear, take a finesse in the suit missing the jack (spades). Since one finesse is as good as the other, you pick up something like an extra 20% by cashing the ♡AK before taking the spade finesse as the ♡Q might fall under the ♡AK. Testing the hearts without giving up the lead has kept you alive to take the spade finesse, not to mention that extra 20%.

Tip

What a difference a spot makes! If declarer has ♠KQ9x then it is right to play off the three top spades first, hoping the jack will drop (37%) and keeping the heart finesse in reserve if it doesn't.

The West hand: ♠J 8 3 2 ♡Q 8 7 ◇2 ♣K Q 10 4 2
The East hand: ♠9 7 5 ♡10 6 5 ◇4 3 ♣A 9 8 6 5

SOLUTION 6

♠ A J 4
♡ J 10
◇ A K J 10
♣ Q 10 9 8

♠ K 10 3 2
♡ K Q
◇ 6 5
♣ A K J 7 6

After you open 1♣ and bid 1♠ over partner's 1◇ response, partner invites slam in clubs, starting with a fourth suit 2♡ bid, and then supporting clubs after you leap to 3NT. You check for keycards and after finding two aces you trot out 6♣, the final contract. The opening lead is the ♡9. East wins the ♡A and returns a heart. Clubs are 2-2. Plan the play.

Your contract depends upon one of two finesses. If either finesse works you don't need the other, but the sad news is that if the finesse you take loses, down you go. Life can be so cruel. There is a way to increase your chances when dealing with two suits each missing a queen, a contract-making finesse being available in either suit. This is the technique to follow after drawing trumps: *play the ace-king of the longer suit*, spades, and if the queen doesn't drop, *take a finesse in the shorter suit*, diamonds. If the diamond finesse works, re-enter your hand and repeat it.

Note: It does not help to play the ◇A and ◇K and then the ◇J. Even if it is covered, you only get one spade discard on the ◇10. That play only wins when the ◇Q is either singleton or doubleton (less than 10%). Besides, you can't afford to play even one round of diamonds as you may need two diamond finesses if the ♠Q doesn't drop. You are much more likely to find the ♠Q singleton or doubleton (close to 20%), the reason for testing spades before taking the diamond finesse.

Warning: This theme (two missing queens) or variations of it will come up again. Forewarned is forearmed.

Tip

When you decide to play the ace-king of a suit that contains ***both the ten and the jack*** *(spades), a suit you have* ***no*** *intention of finessing, at some point lead the jack. You'll be pleasantly surprised how often the jack is covered.*

The West hand: ♠9 7 6 ♡9 8 7 6 ◇Q 7 3 2 ♣5 4
The East hand: ♠Q 8 5 ♡A 5 4 3 2 ◇9 8 4 ♣3 2

SOLUTION 7

♠ K J 10
♡ 10 4 2
◇ J 5 3
♣ A Q J 5

♠ A Q 9 8 4 3
♡ A K J 5
◇ Q 8 2
♣ —

With both sides vulnerable, West opens 1◇, North and East pass, you double, partner responds 3♣ (being too strong to make a forced 2♣ response). You bid 3♠, forcing, and partner raises to 4♠.

West leads the ◇A, ◇K and another diamond. East trumps the third diamond and exits with a low heart. Spades are 2-2. What is your plan? (Notice that the ◇J and ◇Q were worthless.)

Only 12 HCP are missing and West, the opening bidder, is a heavy favorite to have all of them, so play accordingly. Win the ♡A, cross to a spade, play the ♣A, discarding a heart, and trump a club. Return to dummy with a spade and trump another club. If the ♣K appears, use the ♣Q to discard a second heart. If the king doesn't appear, try to drop the ♡Q in the West hand. Why finesse into a player who is known to have the queen?

Tip

When the bidding tells you that a particular defender must have a particular card, play that defender for that card even if it means going against the odds.

Tip

*Assume an opening bidder has at least 12 HCP unless the opener is **known** to have a distributional hand, in which case 10 or 11 HCP is possible.*

The West hand: ♠5 2 ♡Q 8 7 ◇A K 10 6 4 ♣K 10 9
The East hand: ♠7 6 ♡9 6 3 ◇9 7 ♣8 7 6 4 3 2

SOLUTION 8 (*ADVANCED*)

♠ 4 3
♡ K J 8 6 5
◇ A 9 6
♣ A 5 4

♠ A Q
♡ A Q 10 9 4 3
◇ K 5 4 2
♣ 7

After you open 1♡ and partner responds 2NT, Jacoby, you show your singleton club and partner bids 3◇. You bid 4NT, Keycard Blackwood, and land in 6♡. The opening lead is the ♣Q. Hearts are 1-1. Plan the play.

You have a certain diamond loser and a possible spade loser. When dealing with losers in two suits, it is almost always right to start with the longer combined suit providing the suit is unevenly divided. Given that your diamonds are 4-3, you may be able to develop an extra diamond trick if their diamonds are divided 3-3. That extra diamond winner can be used to discard a spade from dummy, thus avoiding the spade finesse.

Win the ♣A, ruff a club high, cross to a trump, ruff dummy's last club and play the ◇A and a low diamond. If East follows with the *lowest* outstanding diamond, play low ducking the trick to West. If West started with a doubleton diamond he will have no safe exit and no spade finesse will be necessary. If West has a diamond exit and diamonds are 4-2, you will need the spade finesse.

If East doesn't play the lowest missing diamond, win the ◇K and exit a diamond hoping they are 3-3 (36%). If you get lucky, you will be able to discard a spade from dummy on your fourth diamond. However, if diamonds are 4-2 (48%), close your eyes and take the spade finesse. Sometimes finesses work. You have a 68% chance of landing this contract by giving yourself two chances.

The normal way to play this combination is to duck a diamond and then play the ◇AK, which allows you to retain control of the suit when the suit breaks 4-2. However, you can't afford to do that here. If you duck a diamond and East wins and returns a spade, you have more or less painted yourself into a corner. You still don't know whether to take the spade finesse or gamble on the diamonds being 3-3. Why put yourself in such a predicament? You must discover how the diamonds break immediately, before East can play a spade through you.

The West hand: ♠K 8 7 6 ♡2 ◇J 8 ♣Q J 8 6 3 2
The East hand: ♠J 10 9 5 2 ♡7 ◇Q 10 7 3 ♣K 10 9

PROBLEM 9

♠ K J 3
♡ K 7 6 4
♢ A J 2
♣ 7 4 3

♠ A Q 2
♡ A 5 2
♢ K Q 8 7
♣ A K J

You open 2♣ and rebid 2NT showing 22 to 24 HCP after partner's 2♢ 'waiting' response. With a perfectly balanced hand, partner disdains Stayman and boosts you to 6NT knowing there are at least 33 HCP between the two hands. The opening lead is the ♠10. Plan the play.

PROBLEM 10

♠ 7 6
♡ 6 5
♢ A 7 6 5 3
♣ A K J 9

♠ A Q J
♡ J 7
♢ K 10
♣ Q 10 8 7 6 5

Partner opens 1♢, you respond 2♣, partner raises to 3♣, and you try 3♠ hoping partner can bid 3NT with a heart stopper. No luck; partner takes you back to 4♣ and you bid 5♣. The opening lead is the ♡K (surprise) and then a heart to East's ♡A. At Trick 3 East shifts to a low spade. Plan the play.

PROBLEM 11 (*ADVANCED*)

♠ A 10 7 6
♡ K 3 2
◇ A 6 2
♣ J 6 3

♠ K Q J 9 8 5
♡ A J 4
◇ 3
♣ K 5 4

West opens 2◇, weak, partner passes, East bids 3◇, you join in with 3♠ and partner is happy to boost you to 4♠. West leads the ◇Q. Plan the play.

PROBLEM 12 (*ADVANCED*)

♠ J 4
♡ Q 10
◇ K Q 7 6 5
♣ J 4 3 2

♠ A 10 8 3
♡ K J 9
◇ A 3 2
♣ A 10 9

After a routine 1NT-3NT, West leads the ♡4 and East plays the ♡2, count. You win the trick in dummy with the ♡10 and can be pretty sure from East's deuce that West has led from ace fifth and East has three small. This is a toughie. Plan the play.

SOLUTION 9

♠ K J 3
♡ K 7 6 4
◇ A J 2
♣ 7 4 3

♠ A Q 2
♡ A 5 2
◇ K Q 8 7
♣ A K J

The opening lead against your 6NT contract is the ♠10. Plan the play.

You have eleven top tricks with two chances for a twelfth: hearts 3-3 (36%) or the ♣Q with East (50%). Once again, trying to set up an extra trick in the longer suit (hearts) is best because if the suit does not break 3-3, you are still alive and can take the club finesse. The plan, therefore, is to duck a heart early. If East wins and plays a club, you win the ♣A and test hearts by playing the ♡A and ♡K. If hearts are 3-3, you won't need the club finesse. Your chance for success is 68%.

The technique of ducking a heart and then later playing the ♡AK is far superior to playing the ♡AK and a third heart to see if they divide 3-3. There are two reasons for this: (1) You retain control of the suit if it breaks 4-2 so you can still take the club finesse; (2) If you play the ♡AK and another heart, and the suit is 4-2, the opponents can take two heart tricks and you never do get a chance to take a club finesse.

You should be able to see the difference between this hand and the previous one. Here it is vital to duck a trick with the very same combination where on Problem 8 it was dangerous to duck a trick. It is risky to play ♡AK and another heart as you may lose two quick tricks if the suit divides 4-2. On this hand your club position is safe from an *immediate* attack so you have time to test the hearts while keeping control of the heart suit.

The West hand: ♠10 9 8 6 ♡10 8 3 ◇10 5 3 ♣Q 9 5
The East hand: ♠7 5 4 ♡Q J 9 ◇9 6 4 ♣10 8 6 2

I have used this hand in my classes for years. One lady who came to all of my classes wound up playing this hand seven or eight times and went down each time; she insisted on taking the club finesse before testing the hearts no matter how much pleading and explaining I did. Finally, the following year, I couldn't stand it any longer and put the ♣Q with East and made hearts 4-2 so she would finally make the hand. This time she won the opening lead and played the ♡AK and a heart allowing them to take two heart tricks. I gave up.

SOLUTION 10

♠ 7 6
♡ 6 5
◇ A 7 6 5 3
♣ A K J 9

♠ A Q J
♡ J 7
◇ K 10
♣ Q 10 8 7 6 5

Partner opens 1◇, you respond 2♣, partner raises to 3♣, and you try 3♠ hoping partner can bid 3NT with a heart stopper. No luck; partner takes you back to 4♣ and you bid 5♣. The opening lead is the ♡K (surprise) and then a heart to East's ♡A. At Trick 3 East shifts to a low spade. Plan the play.

Stick in the ♠Q. A 50% chance is better than trying to set up the diamonds for two spade discards. In order for that to happen, you need diamonds to be 3-3, a 36% chance.

Ideally, you would like to have had time to test the diamonds first, but you didn't have that luxury. You were forced to make an early decision, so knowing the odds helps.

Say you had one fewer spade and one more club and received the same defense. Now you need only one spade discard on dummy's diamonds, not two. In other words, you can make this contract if diamonds divide 3-3 *or* 4-2 (36% + 48%). Given these numbers it is much better to rise with the ♠A and try to set up the diamonds. An 84% chance is better than a 50% chance.

The West hand ♠ 10 8 5 2 ♡K Q 9 3 2 ◇Q 9 ♣ 4 3
The East hand: ♠ K 9 4 3 ♡A 10 8 4 ◇J 8 4 2 ♣ 2

SOLUTION 11 (*ADVANCED*)

♠ A 10 7 6
♡ K 3 2
◇ A 6 2
♣ J 6 3

♠ K Q J 9 8 5
♡ A J 4
◇ 3
♣ K 5 4

West opens 2◇, weak, partner passes, East bids 3◇, you join in with 3♠ and partner is happy to boost you to 4♠. West leads the ◇Q. Plan the play.

After stripping diamonds and drawing trumps, you could take three finesses and if just one of them worked (a rousing 87%) you would make your game. Those three finesses are leading up the ♣K and, if that loses, leading up to the ♣J, and if that loses taking the heart finesse. Could all three finesses lose?

You deserve to go down if you took the 'three finesse line' when there is a 100% line available. After stripping diamonds and drawing trumps, play the ♡A, ♡K and ♡J. If West wins the ♡Q and leads a club, you must take a trick with the ♣K. If East wins the ♡Q and leads a club, play low from your hand and again you have a sure club trick. Either way the most you can lose is two club tricks and your contract is ensured.

Notice you have two equally divided side suits, clubs and hearts. It is more important to throw them in with a heart to force a club play than vice versa. Forcing a club play means you can't possibly lose more than two clubs and one heart. If you throw them in with clubs to force a heart return, you could lose three clubs and a heart (when East wins the third club and West has the ♡Q).

> ***Tip***
> *With touchy side suits (there are oodles), the idea is to force the opponents to lead the suit first.*

> ***Tip***
> *If your **only** losers are in a 'touchy suit' (meaning **you** have to play the suit first), strip the hand, if possible, before attacking the suit. Good things can happen, very good things, wonderful things.*

The West hand: ♠3 ♡Q 9 5 ◇Q J 10 9 7 5 ♣A 8 2
The East hand: ♠4 2 ♡10 8 7 6 ◇K 8 4 ♣Q 10 9 7

SOLUTION 12 (*ADVANCED*)

♠ J 4
♡ Q 10
◇ K Q 7 6 5
♣ J 4 3 2

♠ A 10 8 3
♡ K J 9
◇ A 3 2
♣ A 10 9

After a routine 1NT-3NT, West leads the ♡4 and East plays the ♡2, count. You win the trick in dummy with the ♡10 and can be pretty sure from East's deuce that West has led from ace fifth and East has three small. This is a toughie. Plan the play.

If diamonds divide 3-2, you will *always* make 3NT, but what if they don't? Time for the 'just in case' Plan B. Try a low club to the ♣10 at Trick 2. Say it loses and another low heart comes back. Now you dare not let them in again. Test the diamonds by playing the ◇A and ◇K. If both follow, take your nine tricks. If someone shows out on the second diamond, you'll be glad there was a Plan B. Repeat the club finesse. If you can bring clubs in for three tricks, using dummy's remaining diamond entry to cash the thirteenth club, you have nine tricks without the diamonds.

Tip

If you can keep your long suit (your 'ace in the hole' suit) in reserve and attack another suit first, trying to establish extra needed tricks in case your ace in the hole suit turns out to be a deuce in the hole suit, do it!

Tip

Before eagerly attacking your strongest suit, at least ask yourself what is to become of you if the suit doesn't break evenly? Yes, it's an unpleasant thought, but the road to becoming a better player includes preparing for unpleasant surprises. It can never hurt to have a Plan B. It's like having a strong bench.

The West hand: ♠K 9 5 2 ♡A 8 7 4 3 ◇9 ♣Q 8 6
The East hand: ♠Q 7 6 ♡6 5 2 ◇J 10 8 4 ♣K 7 5

PROBLEM 13 (*ADVANCED*)

♠ K 10 6 5
♡ K J 9 8
◇ A 9
♣ 5 4 2

♠ A J 3 2
♡ A Q 7
◇ 5 4
♣ A 8 7 6

After you open 1NT, a Stayman sequence lands you in 4♠. West leads the ◇Q. Plan the play.

PROBLEM 14 (*ADVANCED*)

♠ 10 8 7 6 5 3
♡ J 7 2
◇ 8 4
♣ 5 3

♠ A
♡ A K Q 10 9
◇ A 6
♣ A K 7 6 2

After you open 2♣ and eventually get heart support, you gamble that you can set up the clubs by trumping one or two in dummy and bid a somewhat optimistic 6♡. West leads the ♠K and there you are. Plan the play.

PROBLEM 15 (*ADVANCED*)

♠ A 9
♡ 8 6 5
♢ 6 5 4 3 2
♣ Q 6 5

♠ J 7 5
♡ A Q 4
♢ A K Q
♣ A K 4 2

You open 2♣ and rebid 2NT after partner responds 2♢. Partner boosts you to 3NT.

West leads the ♠3, fourth highest, and you play low from dummy. East wins the ♠Q and returns the ♠8, West playing the deuce indicating a five-card suit. When you play the ♢A and ♢K, West discards a heart on the second diamond. Plan the play from here. So far, it's been a bit 'rocky'.

PROBLEM 16

♠ 9 7 3
♡ A 9 5 3 2
♢ Q J 10 9
♣ 6

♠ A 5 4
♡ Q J 10 8 7
♢ K 4
♣ A Q 10

After you open 1♡ in fourth seat, partner's leap to 4♡ ends the bidding.

West leads the ♠2, fourth best, to East's ♠K and your ♠A. Now what? Plan the play.

SOLUTION 13 (*ADVANCED*)

♠ K 10 6 5
♡ K J 9 8
◇ A 9
♣ 5 4 2

♠ A J 3 2
♡ A Q 7
◇ 5 4
♣ A 8 7 6

After you open 1NT, a Stayman sequence lands you in 4♠. West leads the ◇Q. Plan the play.

If you guess the right way to finesse for the ♠Q you have ten sure tricks, but if you don't, you have four losers. Rather than put all of your eggs in the ♠Q basket, give yourself an extra chance. See it? Play the ♠A and ♠K. The ♠Q has been known to drop singleton or doubleton (in fact, that will happen 33% of the time). If the ♠Q drops doubleton, draw trumps, pitch a diamond on the fourth heart, concede two clubs, make an overtrick, and go on to the next hand. If it drops singleton, draw trumps and take your ten sure tricks.

If the ♠Q does not come to the party and remains at large, play on hearts. If the player with the ♠Q has at least three hearts, you can discard your losing diamond on the fourth heart. You wind up losing two clubs and a spade, and go on to the next hand.

The opportunity to get home with either the ♠Q coming down in two rounds *or* the player with ♠Qxx having at least three hearts gives you about a 60% chance of success, better than the 'all in one basket' spade finesse.

The West hand: ♠Q 8 7 ♡10 6 3 ◇Q J 10 8 ♣K J 9
The East hand: ♠9 4 ♡5 4 2 ◇K 7 6 3 2 ♣Q 10 3

SOLUTION 14 (*ADVANCED*)

♠ 10 8 7 6 5 3
♡ J 7 2
◇ 8 4
♣ 5 3

♠ A
♡ A K Q 10 9
◇ A 6
♣ A K 7 6 2

After you open 2♣ and eventually get heart support, you gamble that you can set up the clubs by trumping one or two in dummy and bid a somewhat optimistic 6♡. West leads the ♠K and there you are. Plan the play.

You have an inescapable diamond loser and you will have to bring in the club suit. If clubs are 3-3, there will be no problem, but we all know that clubs are more likely to be 4-2 and if they are, there could be trouble — particularly if East, sitting in back of dummy, also has two clubs. You could risk ruffing the first club with the ♡7 hoping East cannot overruff with the ♡8, but you can do better.

It is easier to ruff one club with dummy's ♡J and one *diamond* low in dummy rather than taking the risk of ruffing two clubs. Play the ♣A and ♣K and lead a third at Trick 4. If West follows, discard a diamond, a sure loser in any event. Assuming clubs are 4-2, you will be able to ruff your ◇6 low in dummy and a fourth club with dummy's ♡J.

This technique of discarding a sure loser (the diamond) from dummy on a long suit is something to be on the lookout for. This may later enable dummy to ruff a loser in your short suit safely *low* and trump a loser in your long suit *high*.

Notice that if you ruff the third club with dummy's ♡J and East shows out, you can still survive. Cross to the ◇A and play a fourth club, discarding a diamond. Your fifth club is good so all you have to do is to ruff your remaining diamond in dummy.

You didn't think I was going to let you get away with ruffing a club with the ♡7, did you?

The West hand: ♠K Q J ♡6 4 ◇Q 10 7 2 ♣Q 10 9 4
The East hand: ♠9 4 2 ♡8 5 3 ◇K J 9 5 3 ♣J 8

SOLUTION 15 (*ADVANCED*)

♠ A 9
♡ 8 6 5
◇ 6 5 4 3 2
♣ Q 6 5

♠ J 7 5
♡ A Q 4
◇ A K Q
♣ A K 4 2

You open 2♣ and rebid 2NT after partner responds 2◇. Partner boosts you to 3NT.

West leads the ♠3, fourth highest, and you play low from dummy. East wins the ♠Q and returns the ♠8, West playing the deuce indicating a five-card suit. When you play the ◇A and ◇K, West discards a heart on the second diamond. Plan the play from here. So far, it's been a bit 'rocky'.

Your sure trick count has been reduced to eight after the diamond 'accident'. You need an extra trick from clubs or hearts. Play three top clubs ending in dummy. If clubs are 3-3 you have nine tricks. If not, you are still alive. If West has four clubs, take the heart finesse. But if East has four clubs, return to your hand with a diamond and exit with the ♠J. Why? Because West only has spades and hearts left. The most West can take is three spade tricks and after fun and games are over, West will have to lead a heart smack into your ♡AQ, giving you tricks number eight and nine. You are such a great player.

Most players do not use throw-in plays nearly enough. This is a good example of how to avoid a finesse via a throw-in. You know that West has only hearts and spades left because West has shown out of both clubs and diamonds earlier. (Good thinking.) As long as West doesn't have enough spades to defeat you (you can be pretty sure he doesn't), you will eventually get a heart return into your ♡AQ.

The West hand: ♠K 10 6 3 2 ♡K 9 7 3 2 ◇10 ♣10 9
The East hand: ♠Q 8 4 ♡J 10 ◇J 9 8 7 ♣J 8 7 3

SOLUTION 16

♠ 9 7 3
♡ A 9 5 3 2
◇ Q J 10 9
♣ 6

♠ A 5 4
♡ Q J 10 8 7
◇ K 4
♣ A Q 10

After you open 1♡ in fourth seat, partner's leap to 4♡ ends the bidding.

West leads the ♠2, fourth best, to East's ♠K and your ♠A. Now what? Plan the play.

You are staring at three losers, two spades and the ◇A, not to mention possibly the ♡K. Working with diamonds gives you a 50% shot as they will win and cash their spade tricks, reducing you to the heart finesse.

If you take the heart finesse and it loses, down you go. But wait! What about the club finesse? If that works, you can discard a spade from dummy on the ♣A. But wait! What if the club finesse loses and the heart finesse was working all along?

Both finesses are 50-50 propositions, but rather than guess which finesse to take, remember the magic word, 'combine'! And guess what? There is a two-king combining rule.

If you are dealing with two suits each missing a king and a finesse for either will land you your contract, but you are going down if you take the wrong one, play the ace of the longer suit (in this case, hearts), and if the king doesn't drop, take a finesse in the shorter suit (here, clubs).

The chance of finding the singleton ♡K (26%) *coupled* with taking the club finesse if the ♡K doesn't drop, is your best bet (63%). Also, when you lead a heart to the ♡A, lead the ♡Q. West may be someone who has covered every honor with an honor since birth.

As an aside, the percentage play with ten cards in a suit between your hand and dummy, missing the king, is to finesse rather than play for the drop of the singleton king. The numbers are huge: 74% for the finesse, 26% for the drop. A word to the wise.

The West hand: ♠Q 10 8 2 ♡6 ◇A 8 6 5 ♣J 9 8 3
The East hand: ♠K J 6 ♡K 4 ◇7 3 2 ♣K 7 5 4 2

PROBLEM 17 (*ADVANCED*)

♠ Q J
♡ A J 8 6
♢ A J 4 3
♣ J 10 4

♠ A 10
♡ K Q 5 4 3 2
♢ K 6 2
♣ A Q

After you open 1♡ and partner responds 2NT, Jacoby, it is difficult not to get to 6♡, but it may be difficult to make it! Opening lead: ♡10, East following. Plan the play.

PROBLEM 18

♠ Q 10 3 2
♡ K 6 5
♢ A Q 7
♣ Q 6 5

♠ A K J 8 7 5
♡ A Q 3
♢ 5
♣ A 7 3

Wild horses can't keep you out of 6♠ after partner opens 1♣ and then raises spades. West leads the ♡J. Plan the play.

PROBLEM 19

♠ AJ654
♡ AQ
◇ 32
♣ J832

♠ K32
♡ 8
◇ A95
♣ AKQ1095

After you open 1♣ and jump to 3♣ after partner's 1♠ response, partner leaps to 6♣. West leads the ◇Q. Clubs are 2-1. Plan the play.

PROBLEM 20

♠ 2
♡ 8
◇ AKJ1076
♣ AQ954

♠ AKJ63
♡ QJ4
◇ 32
♣ J107

Partner opens 1◇, you respond 1♠, West overcalls 2♡, partner chimes in with 3♣, and your 3NT bid ends the auction, partner passing reluctantly. West leads the ♡6, East plays the ♡9, and there you are in the wrong contract (partner's fault, of course). Plan the play.

SOLUTION 17 (*ADVANCED*)

♠ Q J
♡ A J 8 6
◇ A J 4 3
♣ J 10 4

♠ A 10
♡ K Q 5 4 3 2
◇ K 6 2
♣ A Q

After you open 1♡ and partner responds 2NT, Jacoby, it is difficult not to get to 6♡, but it may be difficult to make it! Opening lead: ♡10, East following. Plan the play.

Three finesses available! One thing to remember: save finesses in equal length suits, particularly equal length short suits, until the end. In other words, save the spade finesse until the bitter end; maybe even later. It is actually wisest to start with the club finesse because that finesse is headed into the West hand, the hand that cannot attack spades safely. In addition, if the club finesse loses, you have established a club winner for a *diamond* discard, a discard that could be helpful in setting up that suit by trumping a diamond for a possible spade discard.

If the club finesse wins, draw the last trump, and cash the ♣A. If the king doesn't drop, play the ◇A, ◇K and a diamond toward the ◇J (the best play for *three* diamond tricks). It produces three tricks whenever the suit breaks 3-3, whenever West has the ◇Q or whenever East has a doubleton ◇Q. If that doesn't work, take the spade finesse.

If the club finesse loses and a club comes back (as good as anything), win in your hand, enter dummy with a trump, and discard a diamond on the ♣J. Now is the time to play the ◇A and ◇K and trump a diamond. If the ◇J is high, cross to dummy with a trump and discard the ♠10 on it. If the ◇J isn't high, take the dreaded equal length spade finesse. You have done everything in your power to avoid the spade finesse. But guess what? It may work!

Tip:
When considering which of several finesses to take and there is a danger hand (East), do yourself a favor and take the first finesse into the non-danger hand (West).

The West hand: ♠K 9 6 5 3 ♡10 9 ◇10 8 5 ♣K 7 5
The East hand: ♠8 7 4 2 ♡7 ◇Q 9 7 ♣9 8 6 3 2

SOLUTION 18

♠ Q 10 3 2
♡ K 6 5
♢ A Q 7
♣ Q 6 5

♠ A K J 8 7 5
♡ A Q 3
♢ 5
♣ A 7 3

Wild horses can't keep you out of 6♠ after partner opens 1♣ and then raises spades. West leads the ♡J. Plan the play.

With eleven top tricks, you have two chances for a twelfth trick: the diamond finesse (needing West to have the ♢K), or leading up to the ♣Q, also needing West to have the ♣K.

Question: Which finesse to take first?

Answer: *The one that 'keeps you alive' even if it loses.*

If you take the diamond finesse and it loses, you are down even if West has the ♣K.

If you lead up to the ♣Q and it loses to East's ♣K, you can still make the hand if West has the ♢K.

Draw trumps, strip hearts ending in your hand, and lead a low club to the ♣Q. You have a 75% chance of making this contract, needing one of two finesses.

The West hand: ♠4 ♡J 10 9 7 ♢J 9 6 4 2 ♣K J 8
The East hand: ♠9 6 ♡8 4 2 ♢K 10 8 3 ♣10 9 4 2

SOLUTION 19

♠ A J 6 5 4
♡ A Q
◇ 3 2
♣ J 8 3 2

♠ K 3 2
♡ 8
◇ A 9 5
♣ A K Q 10 9 5

After you open 1♣ and jump to 3♣ after partner's 1♠ response, partner leaps to 6♣. West leads the ◇Q. Clubs are 2-1. Plan the play.

You have two suits with finesse possibilities to play around with, spades and hearts, but be reminded, if the opponents get in they will cash a diamond!

If the heart finesse works, you can discard a spade on the ♡A, then probably set up the spades for two diamond discards and an overtrick. If spades cannot be established for two discards, you will concede a diamond and ruff your remaining diamond. Easy enough if the heart finesse works, but what if doesn't? They cash a diamond and down you go — and maybe the spade finesse was right all along!

If the spade finesse works, and the suit breaks 3-2, you have thirteen tricks; even if the suit breaks 4-1, you can concede a diamond, ruff a diamond and make your slam without worrying about who has the ♡K. But if the spade finesse loses, they take a diamond and down you go. So which finesse should you take?

Neither just yet, it was a trick question. You can increase your chances dramatically by playing the ♠A and ♠K to see if the ♠Q drops singleton or doubleton (33%). If it doesn't, take the heart finesse. This must be better than guessing which finesse to take. Besides, testing spades keeps you alive for the heart finesse. Your chance of making the hand on this line is a bit more than 65%, better than taking a spade finesse after cashing the ♠K first. Incidentally, if the contract were 7♣, you should play it the same way.

Tip:

When you can't afford to give up the lead and you have two finesse suits, one missing a queen, the other a king, and you need to pick the right one to make your contract, don't try either! Play the ace-king of the suit missing the queen, and if the queen doesn't drop, try a finesse in the suit missing the king.

The West hand: ♠ 8 7 ♡ K 9 6 3 2 ◇ Q J 8 7 ♣ 6 4
The East hand: ♠ Q 10 9 ♡ J 10 7 5 4 ◇ K 10 6 4 ♣ 7

SOLUTION 20

♠ 2
♡ 8
♢ A K J 10 7 6
♣ A Q 9 5 4

♠ A K J 6 3
♡ Q J 4
♢ 3 2
♣ J 10 7

Partner opens 1♢, you respond 1♠, West overcalls 2♡, partner chimes in with 3♣, and your 3NT bid ends the auction, partner passing reluctantly. West leads the ♡6, East plays the ♡9, and there you are in the wrong contract (partner's fault, of course). Plan the play.

Obviously, you can't give up the lead, and you have two suits to work with, diamonds, a suit missing the queen, and clubs, a suit missing the king. What to do? Remember your 'combining' rule and *stay alive, stay alive!*

Start by cashing the ♢A and ♢K. If the queen drops, you have ten tricks. If it doesn't, cross to the ♠A. No finesse, please! Even if the ♠J were to hold, you would still need the club finesse, so why take a practice (unnecessary) finesse? After winning the ♠A, run the ♣J. If it holds, cash a second spade, discarding a diamond from dummy, and repeat the finesse running the ♣10.

You can use the tip from the last hand on this one as well. It bears repeating: when you can't afford to give up the lead and you have two finesse suits going for you, one missing a queen, the other a king, either suit affording you enough tricks to make your contract if the finesse works, play the ace-king of the suit missing the queen, and if the queen doesn't drop, take a finesse in the suit missing the king.

Your odds of making this hand are the same as in the previous hand (about 65%). You used the same technique but in a slightly different guise.

The West hand: ♠Q 9 5 ♡A K 7 6 5 2 ♢9 8 5 ♣2
The East hand: ♠10 8 7 4 ♡10 9 3 ♢Q 4 ♣K 8 6 3

PROBLEM 21

♠ J 9
♡ K 7 6 2
◇ K J 10 4
♣ K 9 6

♠ A K
♡ A 5 3
◇ A Q 9 5
♣ 8 7 5 4

After you open 1NT, partner responds 2♣ and you wind up in 3NT. West leads the ♠4. East plays the ♠6, standard count. Plan the play.

PROBLEM 22

♠ A 7 2
♡ 4 3
◇ A 8 5 4
♣ A 7 6 5

♠ K Q 6 4
♡ A 2
◇ K 3 2
♣ K J 3 2

An auction of 1NT-3NT gets you the opening lead of the ♡6, East playing the ♡J. Plan the play. (This is Question A.) Question B: Plan the play with the same lead, but this time you have the ◇KJ2 instead of ◇K32?

PROBLEM 23

♠ A Q J
♡ 4 3 2
♢ A 8 4 3
♣ 7 6 5

♠ K 10 9 8
♡ A K Q 5
♢ Q J
♣ Q 9 4

The opponents are getting tired of defending so many 3NT hands, but here comes another 1NT-3NT. West leads a low club from ♣K10xx and the opponents cash the first four club tricks, East discarding a low spade on the fourth club, dummy a low heart. And you, what do you discard on the fourth club?

PROBLEM 24 (*ADVANCED*)

♠ 9 4
♡ 8 3
♢ 8 7 4
♣ A K 8 6 5 4

♠ A K Q J
♡ J 10 9 4
♢ A J 10
♣ 3 2

Partner raises your 1NT opening to 3NT hoping you can use the clubs. West leads a low heart from ♡KQxx and the opponents play four rounds of hearts. You win the fourth round of hearts, East discarding a discouraging spade. What two discards did you make from dummy and what is your plan?

SOLUTION 21

♠ J 9
♡ K 7 6 2
◇ K J 10 4
♣ K 9 6

♠ A K
♡ A 5 3
◇ A Q 9 5
♣ 8 7 5 4

After you open 1NT, partner responds 2♣ and you wind up in 3NT. West leads the ♠4. East plays the ♠6, standard count. Plan the play.

You have eight top tricks with two chances for a ninth: leading up to the ♣K (50%) or playing for 3-3 hearts (36%). Unfortunately, given the fragility of the spade position (you can only let them in one more time before their spades are established) you don't have time to try both. Which will it be?

When one line gives you a 50% chance and the other 36%, guess which one you should take? After cashing four diamonds, lead up to the ♣K.

> ***Tip:***
> *When you don't have 'time' to give yourself two chances in the play, take the one that offers the best odds.*

Notice that East's count card at Trick 1 from the 7652 was *second* highest from four small; the highest card tends to show a doubleton — assuming a doubleton is possible.

The West hand: ♠Q 10 8 4 3 ♡10 8 ◇7 6 3 ♣A J 2
The East hand: ♠7 6 5 2 ♡Q J 9 4 ◇8 2 ♣Q 10 3

SOLUTION 22

♠ A 7 2
♡ 4 3
◇ A 8 5 4
♣ A 7 6 5

♠ K Q 6 4
♡ A 2
◇ K 3 2
♣ K J 3 2

An auction of 1NT-3NT gets you the opening lead of the ♡6, East playing the ♡J. Plan the play. (This is Question A) Question B: Plan the play with the same lead, but this time you have the ◇KJ2 instead of ◇K32?

(A) You have eight top tricks and dare not let them in before you get nine. Win the ♡A and test spades, a suit that allows you to stay alive even if it doesn't break 3-3. If it doesn't, you still have eight tricks. You are now reduced to the club finesse: play the ♣A and low to the ♣J, your best chance for three clubs tricks.

(B) With ◇KJ2, you have *three* chances. Test the spades, again staying alive if they don't break 3-3. If they don't, you still have *two* suits to play around with, both missing a queen, both having finesse possibilities. Which finesse to take? Remember the combining two-queen rule?

When missing a queen in two suits, a finesse possible in either suit, cash the ace-king of the longer suit (clubs) and if the queen doesn't drop, take a finesse in the shorter suit (diamonds). This is a recording.

The West hand (A) ♠ 10 8 3 ♡K 10 8 6 5 ◇10 7 ♣Q 10 9
The East hand (A) ♠J 9 5 ♡Q J 9 7 ◇Q J 9 6 ♣8 4

The West hand (B) ♠ 10 8 ♡K 10 8 6 5 ◇10 7 6 ♣Q 10 9
The East hand (B) ♠J 9 5 3 ♡Q J 9 7 ◇Q 9 3 ♣8 4

SOLUTION 23

♠ A Q J
♡ 4 3 2
◇ A 8 4 3
♣ 7 6 5

♠ K 10 9 8
♡ A K Q 5
◇ Q J
♣ Q 9 4

The opponents are getting tired of defending so many 3NT hands, but here comes another 1NT-3NT. West leads a low club from ♣K10xx and the opponents cash the first four club tricks, East discarding a low spade on the fourth club, dummy a low heart. And you, what do you discard on the fourth club?

If you discard a heart, you are giving up on 3-3 hearts (36%) but if you discard a diamond, you are giving up on the diamond finesse (50%). Discard a heart.

Also, if East had the ◇K, he might have discarded an encouraging diamond. Negative inferences go a long way in this game.

The West hand: ♠5 4 3 ♡J 7 ◇K 6 5 2 ♣K 10 8 2
The East hand: ♠7 6 2 ♡10 9 8 6 ◇10 9 7 ♣A J 3

See the diamonds in your hand? Harold Harkavy, a wonderful bridge player of yesteryear, supported himself by playing professionally. He frequently found himself in some bizarre 3NT contracts because his partners were not allowed to bid notrump. On one of them this was his diamond stopper — only his contract was 4NT!

◇ Q J

◇ A 10 8 3 ◇ K 6 5 4

(Harold)
◇ 9 7 2

Harold had to knock out an ace and knew the opponents would switch to diamonds so he decided to feign strength in diamonds by leading the ◇Q from dummy with great confidence. It held the trick! Undaunted, he led the jack and that held the trick as well! Now it was safe to let the opponents in and Harold made yet another impossible contract. After the hand, he apologized to his partner, saying, 'Partner, if I had only had the ten of diamonds, I could have run the entire suit!'

SOLUTION 24 (*ADVANCED*)

♠ 9 4
♡ 8 3
◇ 8 7 4
♣ A K 8 6 5 4

♠ A K Q J
♡ J 10 9 4
◇ A J 10
♣ 3 2

Partner raises your 1NT opening to 3NT hoping you can use the clubs. West leads a low heart from ♡KQxx and the opponents play four rounds of hearts. You win the fourth round of hearts, East discarding a discouraging spade. What two discards did you make from dummy and what is your plan?

You have eight top tricks with two possibilities for a ninth. You can duck a club and play for 3-2 clubs (68%), or you can give up on clubs (!) and use your two club entries to take two diamond finesses. If East has one or both diamond honors you can secure your ninth trick in that suit. Which is better? What are the numbers, please?

Two diamond finesses is a better line. When you need one of two finesses to work, you have a 75% chance that at least one will succeed. Even though it may kill you to give up on the club suit, 75% is better than 68%. Incidentally, I hope you didn't discard two diamonds from dummy on the third and fourth round of hearts!

Tip:

West's passive heart return at Trick 4 suggests no fear of the club suit. An inference.

The West hand: ♠10 7 5 ♡K Q 6 2 ◇Q 9 ♣Q 10 9 7
The East hand: ♠8 6 3 2 ♡A 7 5 ◇K 6 5 3 2 ♣J

PROBLEM 25

♠ A K 9 3
♡ 9
♢ K 10 9 6 2
♣ A J 10

♠ J 10 2
♡ K 7 3 2
♢ A Q J 8
♣ Q 9

You open 1♢, partner responds 1♠, East joins in with 2♡, you make a support double showing three spades (a raise to 2♠ shows four) and suddenly you find yourself playing 6♢! West leads the ♡5, East wins the ♡A and returns the ♡Q, West following with a ***higher*** heart. How do you proceed? Both follow to the first diamond.

PROBLEM 26 (*ADVANCED*)

♠ A Q 9 6 5 3
♡ K 8
♢ 6 2
♣ 10 9 4

♠ 4 2
♡ —
♢ K J 3
♣ A K Q J 7 6 3 2

Partner opens 2♠, weak, and your leap to 5♣ silences the table. West leads the ♡Q. Plan the play.

PROBLEM 27

♠ 10 9 8
♡ Q J 8 7 5
◇ A J 10
♣ 5 4

♠ 7
♡ A K 10 9 4
◇ K 9 3
♣ A K J 3

After you open 1♡, partner makes a limit raise, you try 4♣, and partner cooperates with 4◇. You check for keycards and discover that partner has an ace and the ♡Q. That's enough for you to bid 6♡. West leads the ♠K, gets an encouraging signal and continues with a low spade to East's ♠A; you trump, making both opponents unhappy. Hearts are 2-1. How do you plan to keep them unhappy?

PROBLEM 28 (*ADVANCED*)

♠ 4 3 2
♡ K 6
◇ K 8 7 4 3 2
♣ 10 5

♠ A Q 7 5
♡ A 5
◇ A Q
♣ A J 9 8 7

Partner opens 2◇, weak, in first chair, a doubtful (some would say diseased) bid. You have seen partner's weak twos before, so you control yourself and sign off by leaping to 3NT. West leads the ♡4. Plan the play.

SOLUTION 25

♠ A K 9 3
♡ 9
◇ K 10 9 6 2
♣ A J 10

♠ J 10 2
♡ K 7 3 2
◇ A Q J 8
♣ Q 9

You open 1◇, partner responds 1♠, East joins in with 2♡, you make a support double showing three spades (a raise to 2♠ shows four) and suddenly you find yourself playing 6◇! West leads the ♡5, East wins the ♡A and returns the ♡Q, West following with a ***higher*** heart. How do you proceed? Both follow to the first diamond.

You have no convenient discard from dummy on the ♡K, so do yourself a favor and ruff the second heart, noticing West's second heart is higher than the ♡5 indicating three hearts. The play now revolves around the best way to tackle the black suits for no losers. Clearly, if either finesse works you make your slam, but which one to take? Surely you are not going to fall for that question any longer.

Start by drawing two rounds of trumps and leading the ♠J hoping for a cover. West may cover hoping partner has the ♠10. If the ♠J isn't covered, win the ♠A and cash the ♠K hoping to drop the ♠Q. If you do, you won't need the club finesse. If you have no luck in spades, return to your hand with a trump and run the ♣Q, your last chance.

Congrats. You didn't put all of your eggs in either basket. You worked with spades hoping to drop the ♠Q, not to mention giving West a chance to err by covering the ♠J. And all the while you had the club finesse in reserve.

Did you notice West's lead of the ♡5 from ♡865 in partner's *unsupported* suit? If West had *supported* hearts, and therefore was known to have at least three of them, the ♡8 would have been the proper lead. After supporting, the lead of the ♡8 should not be confused with a doubleton.

Tip:
Pay attention to the spot card led so when a second card is played in the suit you will know whether it is higher or lower than the first.

The West hand: ♠8 7 5 4 ♡8 6 5 ◇7 4 3 ♣8 6 4
The East hand: ♠Q 6 ♡A Q J 10 4 ◇5 ♣K 7 5 3 2

SOLUTION 26 (*ADVANCED*)

♠ A Q 9 6 5 3
♡ K 8
◇ 6 2
♣ 10 9 4

♠ 4 2
♡ —
◇ K J 3
♣ A K Q J 7 6 3 2

Partner opens 2♠, weak, and your leap to 5♣ silences the table. West leads the ♡Q. Plan the play.

The idea is to set up the spades to discard diamonds without letting East in to lead a diamond. After all, you could lose three tricks in the two suits if East has the ♠K and West the ◇AQ. Another bad news scenario is East winning the ♠K and shifting to a low diamond, putting you to an uncomfortable guess even if the diamond honors are divided.

Unfortunately, the spade finesse goes directly into East and East will surely shift to a diamond. Can you figure out a way to keep East off lead even if East has the ♠K?

Duck the opening lead in dummy and unless East plays the ♡A, discard a spade from your hand! What can West do? In fact, if West doesn't cash the ◇A, it is likely that you will be able to discard all of your diamonds on established spades and make an overtrick. Notice that dummy has three club entries that will help you establish the spades even if the suit breaks 4-1.

In fact, if spades are 4-1, West has to shift to a trump at Trick 2 to kill a needed dummy entry prematurely. If West shifts to a trump at Trick 2 and spades are 4-1 and the ♠K is not singleton, you will have to lead a diamond from dummy and guess what to do if East plays low. I have complete confidence in you. Also, go after West as a partner rather than an opponent in the future.

In order to make this loser-on-loser play at Trick 1, you have to advance the play mentally, so to speak. You have to ask yourself what is likely to happen if the spade finesse loses and a diamond comes back? Some terrifying scenarios can be avoided by looking ahead. With luck, you will frighten yourself into making the winning play!

The West hand: ♠J 7 ♡Q J 10 7 5 2 ◇A Q 7 5 ♣8
The East hand: ♠K 10 8 ♡A 9 6 4 3 ◇10 9 8 4 ♣5

SOLUTION 27

♠ 10 9 8
♡ Q J 8 7 5
◇ A J 10
♣ 5 4

♠ 7
♡ A K 10 9 4
◇ K 9 3
♣ A K J 3

After you open 1♡, partner makes a limit raise, you try 4♣, and partner cooperates with 4◇. You check for keycards and discover that partner has an ace and the ♡Q. That's enough for you to bid 6♡. West leads the ♠K, gets an encouraging signal and continues with a low spade to East's ♠A; you trump, making both opponents unhappy. Hearts are 2-1. How do you plan to keep them unhappy?

Don't you dare put all of your eggs in one finesse basket! After drawing trumps, the way to stay alive is to play the ♣AK and ruff a club. If the ♣Q appears (think 37%), the ♣J is high and can be used to discard a diamond. If the ♣Q remains at large, go fishing for the ◇Q. A 70% chance (at least) is better than a 50% 'too quick' finesse chance.

Tip:

When faced with a two-way finesse for a queen (diamonds), the idea is to try to determine which opponent started with the longer diamonds and play that opponent for the queen. In other words you have to count! If you can't tell, you might as well play the opponent you dislike the most for the queen. Then if the finesse works, it gives you more satisfaction. Good luck!

The West hand: ♠K Q 6 4 2 ♡6 ◇7 6 5 4 ♣Q 10 6
The East hand: ♠A J 5 3 ♡3 2 ◇Q 8 2 ♣9 8 7 2

SOLUTION 28 (*ADVANCED*)

♠ 4 3 2
♡ K 6
◇ K 8 7 4 3 2
♣ 10 5

♠ A Q 7 5
♡ A 5
◇ A Q
♣ A J 9 8 7

Partner opens 2◇, weak, in first chair, a doubtful (some would say diseased) bid. You have seen partner's weak twos before, so you control yourself and sign off by leaping to 3NT. West leads the ♡4. Plan the play.

Well, it certainly looks right to win the ♡A, cash the ◇AQ and eventually cross to the ♡K and run the diamonds. It may look right, but it isn't!

What are you planning to do if diamonds break 4-1? At this point your best chance is to lead a low club to the ♣10, win the heart return with dummy's ♡K, cash the ◇K, and then take a club finesse. Barring a defensive error, you need to find East with the ♣KQ(x). Not good. Beside, it is undignified to go down in a game contract when you were contemplating bidding a slam! Had you thought of the possibility of a 4-1 diamond break (28%, but more for you and me), you might have had a Plan B in reserve.

Plan B: Win the ♡A and play the ◇AQ, but this time overtake the ◇Q with the ◇K! Looks crazy, but it's best. If diamonds break 3-2, give up a diamond and take at least nine tricks: five diamonds, two hearts and two black aces.

Your pickup comes when diamonds are 4-1. Now you have *two* dummy entries to take two club finesses. If the honors are divided and the suit splits 3-3, or East has both honors, you will take four club tricks or nine in all: Four clubs, two diamonds, two hearts and the ♠A. It never hurts to have a Plan B!

The West hand: ♠K 9 ♡Q 8 7 4 ◇J 10 6 5 ♣K 6 4
The East hand: ♠J 10 8 6 ♡J 10 9 3 2 ◇9 ♣Q 3 2

PROBLEM 29 (*ADVANCED*)

♠ K 5 3
♡ K 6 4
♢ J 5
♣ K Q 10 9 5

♠ A Q 7 4
♡ A Q 7 2
♢ A K Q
♣ A 4

You play that an opening bid of 3NT shows 25-26 HCP so that's what you open. Partner, knowing that there are at least 37 HCP between the two hands, possibly 38, signs off in 7NT. West leads the ♢10. Plan the play.

PROBLEM 30

♠ 7 6 5
♡ A Q 6 5
♢ A Q 8
♣ 10 9 8

♠ K 4 3
♡ 3
♢ 4 2
♣ A K Q J 7 6 5

Sometimes things go awry and you get to the wrong contract. Here you wind up in 5♣ instead of 3NT (partner's fault, again) and the opening lead is the ♠2. East wins the ♠A and returns the ♠J to your ♠K. Any clever thoughts?

PROBLEM 31

♠ A Q J
♡ A 5
♢ A 7 6 5 4
♣ K J 9

♠ 9 8
♡ 10 8 6
♢ J
♣ A Q 10 8 7 6 5

You open 3♣ and partner experiments with a new gadget you have decided to play, a jump to 4♢ after a 3♣ opening bid as Keycard Blackwood. The idea is to keep the bidding low as well as having room to make a queen-ask, if necessary. In any case, you wind up in 6♣ and West leads the ♡Q. Clubs are 2-1. Plan the play.

PROBLEM 32 (*ADVANCED*)

♠ 6 4
♡ K Q 3
♢ A K 8 6 3
♣ 9 4 2

♠ A Q
♡ J 6 5 2
♢ 7 5
♣ A K J 10 5

After partner opens 1♢, East overcalls 1♠, you kick in with 2♣ and then leap to 3NT after partner rebids 2♢. West leads the ♠2, East plays the ♠K. Plan the play.

SOLUTION 29 (*ADVANCED*)

♠ K 5 3
♡ K 6 4
◇ J 5
♣ K Q 10 9 5

♠ A Q 7 4
♡ A Q 7 2
◇ A K Q
♣ A 4

You play that an opening bid of 3NT shows 25-26 HCP so that's what you open. Partner, knowing that there are at least 37 HCP between the two hands, possibly 38, signs off in 7NT. West leads the ◇10. Plan the play.

You have twelve top tricks with chances for a thirteenth in three suits. What should your order of plays be? Notice that clubs is a 'two-way' suit. It can be played from the top, ♣A, ♣K, ♣Q, or ♣A and low to the ♣10, the winning play if West started with four clubs.

If possible, two-way suits should be saved until the bitter end. They should be treated the same as finesses in equal length short suits. Later, baby, later. After you play the other suits first, you may have a count on the two-way suit before you attack it.

Start by cashing three diamonds, discarding a club, and then test both major suits hoping for a 3-3 division in at least one of them. If this doesn't happen, you may have enough distributional information to know how to play clubs.

The West hand: ♠ J 8 ♡ 10 9 ◇ 10 9 8 4 2 ♣ J 8 3 2
The East hand: ♠ 10 9 6 2 ♡ J 8 5 3 ◇ 7 6 3 ♣ 7 6

Given this layout, you would know that West started with at least four clubs. How? East has followed to three diamonds and is known to have started with exactly four cards in each major. Ergo, East can have no more than two clubs. Had East started with two diamonds, you would know clubs would be 3-3.

Tip:

Besides being able to get a count on a two-way suit (oftentimes a suit missing a queen that can be finessed in either direction), a relative or a close friend might lead the suit, ending your problems. Now you have two great reasons for postponing the play of a two-way suit for as long as possible.

SOLUTION 30

♠ 7 6 5
♡ A Q 6 5
◇ A Q 8
♣ 10 9 8

♠ K 4 3
♡ 3
◇ 4 2
♣ A K Q J 7 6 5

Sometimes things go awry and you get to the wrong contract. Here you wind up in 5♣ instead of 3NT (partner's fault, again) and the opening lead is the ♠2. East wins the ♠A and returns the ♠J to your ♠K. Any clever thoughts?

If either red suit finesse works, you make your contract, but which one to take? Why not give yourself two chances? Trump a couple of hearts hoping the ♡K appears. It will actually appear about 22% of the time. Not too shabby for a staying alive freebie.

If the ♡K does not drop, take the diamond finesse. When dealing with two possible finesse suits, each missing a king, one having a singleton (hearts), first try to ruff out the king of that suit. If that doesn't work, take the other finesse.

It is hard to construct a bidding sequence on this layout that does not end up in 3NT. Nonetheless, it will be easier to forgive your partner for getting you into this mess if you make the contract.

A reasonable sequence to get to 3NT would be 1♣-1♡, 3♣-3◇, 3NT-pass

If that isn't your cup of tea, maybe this is: 1♣-1♡, 2♣-2◇, 3NT-pass

Notice that the 'third suit,' 3◇ in this sequence, after opener rebids the first suit is not always a true suit. It is often a stopper-showing bid looking for a stopper in the unbid suit for notrump. Typically, the third suit by the responder after having made a one level shows 11+ HCP assuming opener has made a non-forcing rebid of his original suit (like 2♣).

The West hand: ♠Q 10 8 2 ♡K 10 7 ◇J 9 6 5 ♣4 3
The East hand: ♠A J 9 ♡J 9 8 4 2 ◇K 10 7 3 ♣2

SOLUTION 31

♠ A Q J
♡ A 5
◇ A 7 6 5 4
♣ K J 9

♠ 9 8
♡ 10 8 6
◇ J
♣ A Q 10 8 7 6 5

You open 3♣ and partner experiments with a new gadget you have decided to play, a jump to 4◇ after a 3♣ opening bid as Keycard Blackwood. The idea is to keep the bidding low as well as having room to make a queen-ask, if necessary. In any case, you wind up in 6♣ and West leads the ♡Q. Clubs are 2-1. Plan the play.

You have two choices:

1. An immediate 'all in one basket' spade finesse (50%) and get it over with quickly.
2. Try to set up the fifth diamond for a spade discard. This requires 4-3 diamonds (62%). Furthermore, if diamonds break obscenely, you still have the spade finesse in reserve. Suddenly you are up to 81%.

Start with the ◇A and ruff a diamond, cross to the ♣9 and ruff a second diamond. If both opponents have followed to each diamond play, diamonds have divided 4-3 and it's all over but adding up the score. Cross to the ♣J, ruff a third diamond, enter dummy with the ♠A, discard your losing spade on dummy's fifth diamond, concede a heart, and ruff a heart. Admirable.

If you had taken the spade finesse early, and it had lost, you would be dead. You would also be a strong candidate for FA (Finessaholics Anonymous).

The West hand: ♠ 10 7 4 2 ♡ Q J 9 4 ◇ Q 9 8 ♣ 4 3
The East hand: ♠ K 6 5 3 ♡ K 7 3 2 ◇ K 10 3 2 ♣ 2

Note: If clubs had divided 3-0, you would have to give up on diamond establishment and fall back on the spade finesse. Why? In order to use an established diamond, assuming a 4-3 division, you must draw trumps. This means that there will not be a trump left in dummy to trump a heart if you discard a spade on the fifth diamond.

SOLUTION 32 (*ADVANCED*)

♠ 6 4
♡ K Q 3
♢ A K 8 6 3
♣ 9 4 2

♠ A Q
♡ J 6 5 2
♢ 7 5
♣ A K J 10 5

After partner opens 1♢, East overcalls 1♠, you kick in with 2♣ and then leap to 3NT after partner rebids 2♢. West leads the ♠2, East plays the ♠K. Plan the play.

You have six top tricks and have to set up three more without letting the opponents in *twice*. If you attack clubs and the finesse loses, you will have built up only *two* extra club tricks so when the opponents get in with the ♡A you are finished.

If you attack hearts first and the suit breaks 3-3, you have three heart tricks and don't need the club finesse. If hearts do not break 3-3, you still have the club finesse in reserve. So hearts before clubs. Whoa, you can make this hand even if hearts break 4-2 and even if the club finesse loses. See it?

To have the best of both worlds, cross to a diamond and 'slide' a *low* heart by East's presumed ♡A. If East rises, you have nine tricks: three hearts plus two tricks in each of the other suits. If East plays low, win the ♡J and switch your attention to clubs, you sneaky devil, you. Cash the ♣A, cross to a diamond and run the ♣9. Even if the finesse loses, you still have nine tricks: four clubs, two diamonds, two spades and one heart.

The West hand: ♠ 8 5 3 2 ♡ 7 4 ♢ J 9 4 2 ♣ Q 8 3
The East hand: ♠ K J 10 9 7 ♡ A 10 9 8 ♢ Q 10 ♣ 7 6

When missing an ace in an unevenly divided suit plus an honor in a longer suit that may have to be driven out, it may be crucial to 'slide' (steal?) an early trick past the player you think has the ace, giving that player a 'Hobson's Choice'. If East rises with the ace, he gives you an extra trick, and if he ducks, you will switch horses and attack your long side suit, a suit in which you can now afford to lose a trick.

PROBLEM 33 (*ADVANCED*)

♠ K 6 5 3
♡ A J 10 4
♢ K
♣ A Q 7 2

♠ A 4
♡ 6 5 3
♢ A 10 9 8 7
♣ K 6 3

Partner opens 1♣, you respond 1♢, partner rebids 1♡ and you leap to 2NT, invitational. Partner has an easy raise to 3NT. The opening lead is the ♣J. Plan the play.

PROBLEM 34

♠ K J 10 2
♡ 6
♢ K Q J 9 3
♣ A 3 2

♠ Q 9 8 7 6
♡ K J 3
♢ 10 2
♣ K 5 4

You arrive at 4♠ after partner opens 1♢ and leaps to 3♠ over your 1♠ response. The lead is the ♣J, East playing the ♣8, encouraging. Plan the play.

PROBLEM 35 (*ADVANCED*)

♠ A Q
♡ J 10 9
♢ J 10 9 5
♣ K 4 3 2

♠ 7 5 2
♡ K 5 4
♢ A Q 8 3
♣ A Q 6

After a simple 1NT-3NT auction West leads the ♡3 and East plays the ♡8, count. Plan the play.

PROBLEM 36

♠ Q 3 2
♡ A 7 6 4 3
♢ A 8
♣ 9 6 4

♠ A K J 10 7 4
♡ K 2
♢ K 10
♣ A K J

You open 2♣ and discover partner has at least five hearts plus both missing aces not to mention the ♠Q. At this point it is pretty hard to stay out of eight spades! However you control yourself and bid only seven. Now you have to make it with the ♢Q lead. Both follow to the first round of spades. Plan the play.

SOLUTION 33 (*ADVANCED*)

♠ K 6 5 3
♡ A J 10 4
◇ K
♣ A Q 7 2

♠ A 4
♡ 6 5 3
◇ A 10 9 8 7
♣ K 6 3

Partner opens 1♣, you respond 1◇, partner rebids 1♡ and you leap to 2NT, invitational. Partner has an easy raise to 3NT. The opening lead is the ♣J. Plan the play.

You start with eight winners, actually nine — even if clubs don't break 3-3, even if East has both heart honors and even if hearts don't break 3-3! See it?

The key lies in the strength of your diamond intermediates plus the *two* sure side-suit entries to your hand. You can develop a safe ninth trick in diamonds by winning the opening lead in dummy, overtaking the ◇K (the key play), and driving out one diamond honor by leading the ◇10. Win any black suit return in your hand (using up one entry) and lead the ◇9, driving out the remaining diamond honor. Don't look now but your ◇87 are both winners, giving you three diamond tricks or nine tricks in all with zero risk.

This 100% line of play emphasizes the importance overtaking an honor with an honor when the long suit intermediates plus the number of side-suit entries to the hand with the long suit suggest the play. If you don't overtake the ◇K, you could go down on this hand.

The West hand: ♠Q 10 8 ♡8 2 ◇5 3 2 ♣J 10 9 8 4
The East hand: ♠J 9 7 2 ♡K Q 9 7 ◇Q J 6 4 ♣5

SOLUTION 34

♠ K J 10 2
♡ 6
◇ K Q J 9 3
♣ A 3 2

♠ Q 9 8 7 6
♡ K J 3
◇ 10 2
♣ K 5 4

You arrive at 4♠ after partner opens 1◇ and leaps to 3♠ over your 1♠ response. The lead is the ♣J, East playing the ♣8, encouraging. Plan the play.

You are off three aces (unsettling!), and must dispose of your slow club loser before the opponents can get in *twice*. You do not have time to drive out the ♠A as a club will come back and when the defense eventually gets in with a red ace, the setting trick in clubs will be right there on the table to haunt you. You have two choices:

(1) Win the lead in dummy and lead a heart hoping to guess the position if East plays low. If East rises, your troubles are over. Your ♡K provides a parking place for your club loser, and the ♣K the entry to the ♡K. If East plays low, put on your guessing shoes, but there's more to the hand than this.

If East is a strong player, East may duck the ♡A. But if East is not a strong player, East will almost always go up with the ♡A looking at that singleton in dummy. You have to know your customers. In any case, the heart play is in theory at least 50% (guessing correctly if East plays low), but in practice far greater for psychological reasons.

(2) Win the club lead in your hand and drive out the ◇A, win the club return in dummy, and play a second and third diamond hoping the suit divides 3-3 (36%). If it does, you can discard your losing club on a third diamond. Percentage-wise it is clearly better to win the opening lead in dummy and lead a heart.

Tip:
This hand illustrates how important it is not to play too quickly to the first trick from either dummy or your hand because of entry considerations. Also, how timing enters into the calculations when you have a slow loser. And, finally, how important it is to know the skill level of each opponent.

The West hand: ♠A ♡Q 9 8 5 2 ◇8 6 5 4 ♣J 10 9
The East hand: ♠5 4 3 ♡A 10 7 4 ◇A 7 ♣Q 8 7 6

SOLUTION 35 (*ADVANCED*)

♠ A Q
♡ J 10 9
♢ J 10 9 5
♣ K 4 3 2

♠ 7 5 2
♡ K 5 4
♢ A Q 8 3
♣ A Q 6

After a simple 1NT-3NT auction West leads the ♡3 and East plays the ♡8, count. Plan the play.

Judging from the lead and East's count signal at Trick 1, West has led from a five-card suit headed by the ♡AQ and East has a doubleton. East is the danger hand, but fortunately the diamond finesse goes into West.

If the diamond finesse works, you have nine tricks and if clubs break 3-3, you have ten. That's the optimistic way of looking at this hand. But what if the diamond finesse loses and the inevitable spade is returned, the other way of looking at this hand. You are now stuck on eight tricks and need clubs to be 3-3 or the spade finesse to work to make your contract. However, if you haven't tested clubs first, you are in a pickle — of your own making.

The answer is to test the clubs *before* taking the diamond finesse. Play three rounds of clubs ending in dummy. If clubs are 3-3, you have nine tricks even if the diamond finesse loses and you won't have to sweat out a spade return. If clubs do not break 3-3 and the diamond finesse loses and a spade comes back, take the finesse. If the spade finesse loses, a club gets cashed, and a heart comes back, you are going down three! Cheer up. You played the hand beautifully.

The West hand: ♠K J 10 ♡A Q 7 3 2 ♢K 4 2 ♣9 8
The East hand: ♠9 8 6 4 3 ♡8 6 ♢7 6 ♣J 10 7 5

Tip:
Watch the opening lead and third hand's Trick 1 signal like a hawk. The distribution of that suit can determine your line of play.

Tip:
When you can see that if a finesse loses a likely return is going to put you to an agonizing guess, consider testing another suit before taking the finesse. What happens in the 'other suit' may help relieve that agonizing guess.

SOLUTION 36

♠ Q 3 2
♡ A 7 6 4 3
♢ A 8
♣ 9 6 4

♠ A K J 10 7 4
♡ K 2
♢ K 10
♣ A K J

You open 2♣ and discover partner has at least five hearts plus both missing aces not to mention the ♠Q. At this point it is pretty hard to stay out of eight spades! However you control yourself and bid only seven. Now you have to make it with the ♢Q lead. Both follow to the first round of spades. Plan the play.

You have twelve top tricks with a possible thirteenth if you can develop a long heart in dummy. To do that, you need hearts to be 3-3 or 4-2, a whopping 84%. The club finesse, a dreaded finesse in an equally divided suit, will also be available if the second heart doesn't get trumped. (If you draw three rounds of trumps, you won't have enough dummy entries if hearts break 4-2.) In any case, it is not likely that this tragedy (an opponent with three spades will have a singleton heart) will befall you. Besides, I wouldn't do that to you because I want you to enjoy this book!

Win the ♢K, preserving the ♢A as a later entry to the North hand (the hand with the side suit you are planning to establish) and play the ♠A and ♠J. Whether spades break 2-2 or 3-1, play the ♡AK and trump a heart high. Assuming hearts are no worse than 4-2, you are home without the club finesse. Cross to the ♠Q, ruff another heart, and cross to the ♢A, your carefully preserved entry to the established heart, allowing you to discard the ♣J.

If hearts are 5-1 (and you escape a second-round heart ruff), you will have to fall back on the club finesse after cashing the ♣A. All your grand slams should be this good.

> ***Tip:***
> *Always choose long-suit establishment, entries permitting, over taking a finesse, particularly when the finesse can be taken later if the long suit doesn't set up.*

The West hand: ♠8 6 5 ♡10 8 ♢Q J 9 6 ♣Q 10 3 2
The East hand: ♠9 ♡Q J 9 5 ♢7 5 4 3 2 ♣8 7 5

PROBLEM 37

♠ A K 6
♡ 9 4 3 2
◇ 4 3 2
♣ A Q 9

♠ 7 2
♡ A Q 7 6 5
◇ A Q
♣ K J 10 4

Partner opens 1♣, raises your 1♡ response to 2♡, later cuebids spades, and you wind up in a rather 'tenuous' 6♡ contract. It's not your fault that the contract is rather tenuous. A good partner would have stronger hearts. West leads the ♠7. Plan the play.

PROBLEM 38

♠ 6 4 2
♡ A 9 2
◇ K J 10 9
♣ K 9 2

♠ A Q 5
♡ J
◇ A Q 8 6 4 3
♣ A Q 8

After you open 1◇ and partner gives you a limit raise (in theory showing five diamonds), you land in 6◇. Yes, partner owes you a diamond, but has compensating values, like perfect fitting honors in hearts and clubs. In any case, you don't plan to say word one — unless you go down! If you make the hand, you will praise partner for breaking the rules. It's important to be covered. West leads the ♡K. Trumps are 2-1. Plan the play.

PROBLEM 39

♠ A 10 2
♡ A K 8 7 5
◇ J 9 8
♣ 10 2

♠ K Q J 9 8 7
♡ 10 2
◇ 6 5 3
♣ A Q

You crawl into 4♠ after partner responds 2♡ to your opening 1♠ bid and raises your 2♠ rebid to 4♠. West leads the ◇K, ◇Q, and ◇10 to East's ◇A and East exits with the expected low club. Plan the play.

PROBLEM 40

♠ K 8
♡ A K Q 9
◇ J 8 7 6
♣ 9 5 4

♠ A Q 6
♡ J 10 5
◇ 10 9 3
♣ A Q 7 2

You open 1♣ and rebid 1NT over partner's 1♡ response. Partner boosts you to 3NT and the opening lead is the ♠2. Plan the play.

SOLUTION 37

♠ A K 6
♡ 9 4 3 2
◇ 4 3 2
♣ A Q 9

♠ 7 2
♡ A Q 7 6 5
◇ A Q
♣ K J 10 4

Partner opens 1♣, raises your 1♡ response to 2♡, later cuebids spades, and you wind up in a rather 'tenuous' 6♡ contract. It's not your fault that it is rather tenuous. A good partner would have stronger hearts. West leads the ♠7. Plan the play.

In order to 'get a handle' on this hand featuring two red-suit finesses, keep in mind the only way to secure *five* heart tricks is to find the ♡Kx with East. However, the safety play for *four* heart tricks is to lead the ♡A, protecting against a singleton ♡K with West. If both opponents follow and the ♡K doesn't appear, enter dummy and lead a heart towards the ♡Q. This works any time the suit is divided 2-2 , East has the ♡K, or West the blank ♡K.

So how many heart tricks do you need? You won't know until you take the diamond finesse! If the finesse loses, you need five heart tricks so lead low to the ♡Q. If the finesse wins, you need four, so you can afford to cash the ♡A first.

The West hand: ♠Q J 10 8 4 ♡K ◇10 8 6 5 ♣8 6 3
The East hand: ♠9 5 3 ♡J 10 8 ◇K J 9 7 ♣7 5 2

This is typical of hands where the play of one suit depends upon the loser count in another suit. Here is another example:

♡ A J 3 2

♡ K 9 5 4

Your contract is 6♡ and another finesse in a safe side suit must be taken sooner or later. If you need *four* heart tricks, lead low to the ♡J, catering to a possible singleton ♡Q with West as well as ♡Qx(x). If East has the singleton ♡Q, you cannot take four tricks. However, the safety play for *three* tricks, guarding against ♡Q10xx in *either* hand, is to cross to the ♡A and lead low — playing the ♡9 if East follows low. If the ♡9 loses, hearts are 3-2 so you have three tricks. If East plays the ♡10 you win it, and when West shows out, drive out the ♡Q. If East shows out, rise with the ♡K and lead low to the ♡J. Once again you score three heart tricks.

In order to play hearts 'properly', take the other finesse first.

SOLUTION 38

♠ 6 4 2
♡ A 9 2
◇ K J 10 9
♣ K 9 2

♠ A Q 5
♡ J
◇ A Q 8 6 4 3
♣ A Q 8

After you open 1◇ and partner gives you a limit raise (in theory showing five diamonds), you land in 6◇. Yes, partner owes you a diamond, but has compensating values, like perfect fitting honors in hearts and clubs. In any case, you don't plan to say word one — unless you go down! If you make the hand, you will praise partner for breaking the rules. It's important to be covered. West leads the ♡K. Trumps are 2-1. Plan the play.

The only suit with a loser(s) is spades and it is an equally divided suit. Your first thought should be to postpone playing spades as long as possible. However, it would be ideal if you could force West to lead a spade smack into your ♠AQ, wouldn't it? Perhaps a loser-on-loser play is in your future?

Win the ♡A, ruff a low heart high, draw trumps, cash three clubs ending in dummy, and lead the ♡9. If East doesn't cover (West may have led from ♡ KQ10 or East might have fallen asleep holding the ♡10), discard a spade. Upon winning the trick West must either return a spade into the ♠AQ or give you a ruff and sluff. Either way you have the rest.

If West happens to give you a ruff and sluff, ruff in dummy, the hand with the longer remaining spades, and discard the ♠Q from your hand, the hand with the shorter remaining spades; the tried and true way to handle a ruff and sluff.

If East produces the ♡10 (bummer), ruff, cash the ♠A, cross to a trump and lead a spade to the ♠Q. You still make the hand if East has the ♠K, but you also make the hand if West started with ♠Kx. West will be endplayed upon winning the trick.

If the spades were reversed (♠AQ5 in dummy and ♠642 in your hand), you would try to strip the hand and throw *East* in by leading a loser from your hand or dummy and discarding a spade from the other hand. Not applicable on this hand unless East has shown powerful hearts and can be thrown in with the ♡9.

The West hand: ♠ K 10 7 3 ♡ K Q 10 8 ◇ 5 2 ♣ 10 5 3
The East hand: ♠ J 9 8 ♡ 7 6 5 4 3 ◇ 7 ♣ J 7 6 4

SOLUTION 39

♠ A 10 2
♡ A K 8 7 5
◇ J 9 8
♣ 10 2

♠ K Q J 9 8 7
♡ 10 2
◇ 6 5 3
♣ A Q

You crawl into 4♠ after partner responds 2♡ to your opening 1♠ bid and raises your 2♠ rebid to 4♠. West leads the ◇K, ◇Q, and ◇10 to East's ◇A and East exits with the expected low club. Plan the play.

The club finesse is a 50-50 shot. However, setting up the hearts for a club discard, needing no worse than 4-2 hearts, logs in at 84%.

Warning: When setting up a long suit, side entries to the hand with the long suit must be conserved. And there must be enough of them. If hearts are a likely 4-2, you will need *two* dummy entries *outside* hearts to set up the suit: one to get over there to ruff the fourth round of hearts and one to get back to dummy to use the established fifth heart after drawing trumps. If you don't have the necessary entries, forget long-suit establishment and try something else.

Win the ♣A, cash a high spade from your hand, leaving two trump entries in dummy, and then cash the ♡AK and ruff a heart. Assuming 4-2 hearts, return to dummy with a spade, ruff a heart high setting up the fifth heart, and cross back to a spade to discard the ♣Q on the long heart. Beautiful.

The West hand: ♠6 4 ♡Q J 6 4 3 ◇K Q 10 ♣J 9 8
The East hand: ♠5 3 ♡9 ◇A 7 4 2 ♣K 7 6 5 4 3

What happened? East ruffed the second heart and cashed the ♣K, down two and the club finesse was onside all along! Why am I so mean to you? I wasn't. You played the hand properly. Only someone who misplayed the hand *badly* and took the club finesse made it. For shame if you made this hand!

SOLUTION 40

♠ K 8
♡ A K Q 9
◇ J 8 7 6
♣ 9 5 4

♠ A Q 6
♡ J 10 5
◇ 10 9 3
♣ A Q 7 2

You open 1♣ and rebid 1NT over partner's 1♡ response. Partner boosts you to 3NT and the opening lead is the ♠2. Plan the play.

With spades apparently 4-4, the safe line with eight top tricks is to develop a ninth in diamonds, not clubs. Why diamonds? Given a normal lie of the cards you will lose three diamonds and a spade. If you try for three club tricks instead, you are going to need the ♣K with East and clubs 3-3 (a whopping 18%).

Win the ♠K in dummy, lead a low diamond to the ten and continue playing diamonds each time you are in. Assuming spades are 4-4, you will lose three diamonds and one spade not having to rely on a miracle club holding.

Tip:

*If you have ample time, develop tricks in suits that have **inevitable** losers, suits missing an ace, an ace-king, or even an ace-king-queen. Why increase your sure loser count by attacking other suits? Play like an expert.*

The West hand: ♠J 9 3 2 ♡8 3 2 ◇A Q 2 ♣K 8 6
The East hand: ♠10 7 5 4 ♡7 6 4 ◇K 5 4 ♣J 10 3

PROBLEM 41 (*ADVANCED*)

♠ A 10 2
♡ K 4 3 2
◇ 9 8 7
♣ A Q J

♠ K Q J 9 8 6
♡ A J 5
◇ K 10
♣ K 5

Partner opens 1♣, you make a strong jump shift to 2♠ and partner raises to 3♠. Blackwood tells you an ace is missing so you sign off in 6♠. West leads the ♣10 and East plays the deuce. Plan the play.

PROBLEM 42

♠ K 6
♡ A 3 2
◇ A Q 5 4 2
♣ J 5 2

♠ A Q J 10 9 2
♡ K J 5
◇ 9 3
♣ 7 3

You respond 1♠ to partner's 1◇ opening bid and leap to 4♠ after partner rebids 1NT.

West starts out with the ♣K, ♣Q, and a third club to East's ♣A. You ruff and lead a diamond to the ◇Q trying to set up a diamond for a heart discard while dummy still has side suit entries. East wins, otherwise this hand wouldn't be in this book, and exits with a low heart. Plan the play.

PROBLEM 43

♠ 10 5
♡ A 10 9 8
♢ 10 8 4
♣ K J 10 9

♠ Q J 8
♡ K Q J
♢ A K 9 7 3
♣ Q 4

You open 1♢, West overcalls 1♠, partner makes a negative double, and you leap to 2NT showing 18-19 HCP, bidding as if partner had responded 1♡. Partner raises to 3NT. West leads the ♠7. Which spade do you play from dummy, or is it a trick question and it doesn't matter? Plan the play.

PROBLEM 44

♠ Q J 9 8
♡ A 4
♢ J 8 6 5
♣ A Q 3

♠ A K 10 3 2
♡ K Q 5
♢ Q 7 4
♣ 5 4

Partner opens 1♢ and raises your 1♠ response to 2♠. You have an easy 4♠ bid and the opening lead from a strong player is the ♣2. Plan the play.

SOLUTION 41 (*ADVANCED*)

♠ A 10 2
♡ K 4 3 2
◇ 9 8 7
♣ A Q J

♠ K Q J 9 8 6
♡ A J 5
◇ K 10
♣ K 5

Partner opens 1♣, you make a strong jump shift to 2♠ and partner raises to 3♠. Blackwood tells you an ace is missing so you sign off in 6♠. West leads the ♣10 and East plays the deuce. Plan the play.

You have eleven top tricks with chances for a twelfth in both red suits. If you take a heart finesse and it loses, down you go as they can cash the ◇A. If you lead up to the ◇K and it loses, they can take a second diamond trick. How about some combining?

Actually you have three chances to make this slam. Draw two rounds of trumps, keeping a trump entry in dummy, and play the ♡AK.

Chance #1: The ♡Q will be singleton or doubleton (nearly 20%).

Chance #2: If that doesn't happen play two more clubs, discarding a heart, and ruff a heart. If hearts are 3-3 (36%), you have established a long heart in dummy for a diamond pitch.

Chance #3: If none of this works out, cross to dummy with a trump and lead a diamond to the ◇K needing East to have the ◇A (50%).

You can't add them all together (you'd get more than 100%!) but your total chance for success is around 75%, which isn't too shabby.

Notice how long you stayed alive before leading a diamond.

The West hand: ♠5 4 3 ♡Q 8 ◇A Q 5 ♣10 9 8 7 3
The East hand: ♠7 ♡10 9 7 6 ◇J 6 4 3 2 ♣6 4 2

SOLUTION 42

♠ K 6
♡ A 3 2
◇ A Q 5 4 2
♣ J 5 2

♠ A Q J 10 9 2
♡ K J 5
◇ 9 3
♣ 7 3

You respond 1♠ to partner's 1◇ opening bid and leap to 4♠ after partner rebids 1NT. West starts out with the ♣K, ♣Q, and a third club to East's ♣A. You ruff and lead a diamond to the ◇Q trying to set up a diamond for a heart discard while dummy still has side suit entries. East wins, otherwise this hand wouldn't be in this book, and exits with a low heart. Plan the play.

Well, you can stick in the ♡J and if it holds you have ten tricks, but what if it is covered? Now you must use your ♡A — the dummy entry you need to set up diamonds. You have put all of your eggs in the heart finesse basket, the wrong basket. You will go down if West has the ♡Q even if diamonds are 3-3 or 4-2 — you won't be able to draw trumps *ending in dummy* after the diamonds set up.

The stronger play is the ♡*K* followed by the ◇A and a diamond ruff. If diamonds are 3-3, draw trumps and discard a losing heart on a winning diamond using the ♡A as the final dummy entry. If diamonds are 4-2, cross to the ♠K and trump another diamond, setting up dummy's fifth diamond. Now draw trumps and hope spades are 3-2. If they are, dummy's fifth diamond will provide a resting place for your losing heart, the ♡A being the entry to wrap it all up.

This line of play basically requires spades to be 3-2 (68%) if diamonds are 4-2 since you are going to have to trump three times in your hand (two diamonds and a club). However, if diamonds are 3-3, you can even handle 4-1 spades. But you do come home lame if diamonds are 5-1 (15%) and the ♡Q was with East all along. Nonetheless, the play of the ♡K at Trick 5 is *far and away* a better play than sticking in the ♡J or playing low.

The West hand: ♠8 7 3 ♡Q 9 8 ◇10 8 7 6 ♣K Q 10
The East hand: ♠5 4 ♡10 7 6 4 ◇K J ♣A 9 8 6 4

Tip:
When setting up a long suit, use dummy's trump entry (or entries) to trump the long suit, saving the side-suit entry for last (here, use the ♠K before the ♡A).

SOLUTION 43

♠ 10 5
♡ A 10 9 8
◇ 10 8 4
♣ K J 10 9

♠ Q J 8
♡ K Q J
◇ A K 9 7 3
♣ Q 4

You open 1◇, West overcalls 1♠, partner makes a negative double, and you leap to 2NT showing 18-19 HCP, bidding as if partner had responded 1♡. Partner raises to 3NT. West leads the ♠7. Which spade do you play from dummy, or is it a trick question and it doesn't matter? Plan the play.

It is not a trick question and it matters. The Rule of 11 tells you that East has no spade higher than the seven, so play the ♠10 from dummy as you may need two dummy entries to work with the diamonds. Patience.

After winning the opening lead, you have seven sure tricks. If you knew spades were 4-4, you could drive out the ♣A and be done with it. However, spades are not 4-4. West figures to have five or six spades, and if you even think of touching a club, someone will grab the ace followed by spades, spades, and more spades.

No, you can't mess with clubs, it has to be diamonds, diamonds, diamonds, and you can't afford to lose a diamond trick. This is getting a bit hairy. The best play in diamonds to avoid a loser is to play East for *both* honors. At Trick 2 run the ◇10. Assuming the ◇10 wins, lead the ◇8. If this is covered, win the ◇K and if West discards, cash four heart tricks and repeat the diamond finesse. Ten tricks.

You have just brought in a 25% game needing two missing honors to be in the same hand, two out of two finesses. However, 25% is better than 0% which is what you have if you attack clubs, or something like 6% if you play the ◇A hoping to snatch a singleton honor from West followed by four heart winners followed by running the ◇10 finessing East for the other honor.

Notrump play often revolves around the number of tricks the opponents can take once they get in. If you can afford to give up the lead to set up extra needed tricks (here, by driving out the ♣A), do it! If you can't afford to give up the lead, you may have to take a risky finesse or two in a suit or suits in which you have the ace. *Play to make, and good luck — you are going to need it!*

The West hand: ♠A K 9 7 3 2 ♡3 2 ◇2 ♣A 8 7 6
The East hand: ♠6 4 ♡7 6 5 4 ◇Q J 6 5 ♣5 3 2

SOLUTION 44

♠ Q J 9 8
♡ A 4
♢ J 8 6 5
♣ A Q 3

♠ A K 10 3 2
♡ K Q 5
♢ Q 7 4
♣ 5 4

Partner opens 1♢ and raises your 1♠ response to 2♠. You have an easy 4♠ bid and the opening lead from a strong player is the ♣2. Plan the play.

Don't tell me you went for that 'strong player' bit as if the lead could be from the king. Well, it could be from the king, but why take a 50% play when you have a 100% play (unless spades are 4-0)?

Win the ♣A, draw trumps, play three rounds of hearts discarding a club from dummy. You are left with one club in your hand and one club in dummy, and now you exit with a club. Whoever has the ♣K must break diamonds, limiting your losses in that suit to two tricks. If you get a ruff and sluff instead of a diamond shift, ruff in dummy and discard a diamond from your hand. Now the most you can lose is two diamond tricks.

This hand would be easier to play if North had the ♣Axx, as temptation would not enter into the picture. This diamond combination is one you definitely want the opponents to lead first. A throw-in play in an equally-divided side suit (clubs will be an equally-divided suit after you discard one from dummy) after the hand has been stripped is a sure-fire way to achieve this.

Sometimes you have to make an unequally-divided side suit (clubs) an equally-divided side suit to prepare for a strip and throw-in play. Be on the lookout for this 'evening-out' process on hands where trumps can be drawn and you will still have trumps in each hand at the time of the throw-in.

The West hand: ♠5 4 ♡10 7 3 2 ♢A 10 9 ♣J 9 7 2
The East hand: ♠7 6 ♡J 9 8 6 ♢K 3 2 ♣K 10 8 6

PROBLEM 45 (*ADVANCED*)

♠ 3
♡ A J 10 9 6 4
◇ A K 5
♣ 10 8 3

♠ K J 9
♡ Q 2
◇ Q J 6 4
♣ A Q 9 4

After partner opens 1♡ and repeats hearts after your 2♣ response, you leap to 3NT, ending the bidding. If partner had continued with 4♣ over your 3NT bid, you would have bid 4♡, arriving at a better contract. Something you may have to mention in the postmortem if 3NT suffers an unhappy fate. The opening lead is the ♠6 and East plays the ♠10. Plan the play in 3NT and forget 4♡!

PROBLEM 46

♠ A Q 6 4 3 2
♡ —
◇ 7 5 4
♣ A K J 6

♠ K J 10 9 8
♡ K 5 2
◇ A Q 3 2
♣ 2

After East passes, you open 1♠, and partner gets excited and leaps to 6♠! No science here. The opening lead is the ♡Q. Plan the play.

PROBLEM 47 (*ADVANCED*)

♠ 7 4 2
♡ A 9 8
♢ Q 9 3
♣ A 10 5 4

♠ A 10 8
♡ —
♢ A K 10 8 7 6 2
♣ Q 3 2

West opens 1♡, East raises to 3♡, preemptive, you join in with 4♢ and partner raises you to 5♢. The opening lead is the ♡Q. Diamonds are 2-1. Plan the play.

PROBLEM 48 (*ADVANCED*)

♠ A Q 3
♡ —
♢ 8 7 6 5 3 2
♣ 8 6 3 2

♠ K 10
♡ A K Q
♢ A Q J
♣ A K 10 9 7

You like your hand, in fact you love it, and open 2♣. Partner bids 2♢, waiting, and you bid 3♣, natural. Once partner supports clubs and later shows an ace, but denies the ♣Q in response to Keycard Blackwood, you have no qualms about bidding 6♣.

West leads the ♡10. You win, discarding a diamond from dummy, and plunk down the ♣A dropping the ♣Q from West. What now? Plan the play.

♠ 3
♡ A J 10 9 6 4
◇ A K 5
♣ 10 8 3

♠ K J 9
♡ Q 2
◇ Q J 6 4
♣ A Q 9 4

After partner opens 1♡ and repeats hearts after your 2♣ response, you leap to 3NT, ending the bidding. If partner had continued with 4♣ over your 3NT bid, you would have bid 4♡, arriving at a better contract. Something you may have to mention in the postmortem if 3NT suffers an unhappy fate. The opening lead is the ♠6 and East plays the ♠10. Plan the play in 3NT and forget 4♡!

It's the old 'not putting all your eggs in one basket' line again. If you take the heart finesse and West has the ♡K you take oodles of tricks, possibly all thirteen. But if East has the ♡K, it is the opponents who are going to take oodles of tricks.

A better idea is to take two club finesses through East, the danger hand. This line ensures three tricks if the honors are divided and will produce four tricks if East has both honors. This line logs in at 75% (one of two finesses) — better, and safer, than the 50-50 proposition of the heart finesse into that villain, East.

After winning with the ♠J, cross to the ◇K and run the ♣8, allowing you next to play the ♣10 and drop the ♣9 under it to retain the lead in dummy, if necessary. Say the ♣8 loses to the ♣J and a heart comes back. Don't change horses in midstream! Win the ♡A and run the ♣10. If this loses, and a heart comes back to East's ♡K and the nightmare continues with a spade return, remember, down three or four is good bridge as long as you played the hand correctly — something else you may have to tell partner.

Tip:
*West knows from East's play of the ♠10 at Trick 1 that you have the ♠KJ9. Therefore, if West gets in, West will not bang down the ♠A in the hopes of catching a blank ♠K in your hand. It is important to know what **they** know about your hand.*

Matchpoint players might opt to go for broke and take the heart finesse on this one. Playing IMPs or rubber bridge, the club suit is the way to go.

The West hand: ♠ A Q 8 6 2 ♡ 8 5 ◇ 9 7 3 2 ♣ J 2
The East hand: ♠ 10 7 5 4 ♡ K 7 3 ◇ 10 8 ♣ K 7 6 5

SOLUTION 46

♠ A Q 6 4 3 2
♡ —
♢ 7 5 4
♣ A K J 6

♠ K J 10 9 8
♡ K 5 2
♢ A Q 3 2
♣ 2

After East passes, you open 1♠, and partner gets excited and leaps to 6♠! No science here. The opening lead is the ♡Q. Plan the play.

You have to avoid two diamond losers even when West has the ♢K. One possibility is to ruff the opening lead, draw trumps and take the club finesse. If it wins, pitch two diamonds on the ♣AK and take the diamond finesse for the overtrick. If the club finesse loses, you still have the diamond finesse available as you can discard two diamonds on clubs. One of two finesses is 75%, not bad.

But 75% doesn't compare to essentially 100%. Discard a diamond from dummy at Trick 1. Say East wins and shifts to a diamond. Sorry, East, too late. Win the ♢A, draw trumps, pitch dummy's remaining diamond on the ♡K, and claim. You lose one heart trick, period. You have exchanged a heart loser you didn't have for two diamond losers you might have had. (If West ruffs East's diamond return, consider switching to gin rummy or sudoku.)

When LHO leads a suit, dummy is void, and you have the second or second and third highest cards in the suit, sometimes you can discard a loser from dummy rather than trumping. This play allows you to discard another slow loser(s) later after you lose the first trick to the ace.

The West hand: ♠5 ♡Q J 10 9 3 ♢K J 8 ♣9 5 4 3
The East hand: ♠7 ♡A 8 7 6 4 ♢10 9 6 ♣Q 10 8 7

The loser-on-loser play works the same when you have a void, RHO leads the suit and dummy has second-round or second- and third-round control of the suit.

♠ 10 4 3

♠ Q J 9 8 2 ♠ A 7 6 5

(You)
♠ K

Hearts are trumps and West leads the ♠Q to East's ♠A and your ♠K. If East returns a spade, dummy's ♠10 is the second highest spade. Discard a loser and after West wins the ♠J you can discard another loser on the ♠10.

SOLUTION 47 (*ADVANCED*)

♠ 7 4 2
♡ A 9 8
◇ Q 9 3
♣ A 10 5 4

♠ A 10 8
♡ —
◇ A K 10 8 7 6 2
♣ Q 3 2

West opens 1♡, East raises to 3♡, preemptive, you join in with 4◇ and partner raises you to 5◇. The opening lead is the ♡Q. Diamonds are 2-1. Plan the play.

You have ten top tricks and must work with the clubs to make this hand, but how? The 'book' way to attack clubs for *three* tricks is to start by leading low to the ♣Q, and if that loses, lead low to the ♣10. However, the person who wrote the 'book' was not at the table during the bidding. The bidding often alters the book way to play a suit. It does here.

You have 23 HCP between your hand and dummy. The opening lead marks East with the ♡K, and from the non-spade lead you can infer that West does not have the ♠KQJ. Therefore, East has at least one spade honor. In any case, East has at least 4 of the missing 17 HCP so West must have the ♣K to justify an opening bid. This will help in the play.

Ruff the opening lead, draw two rounds of trumps ending in your hand, and lead a club to the ♣10. If West has both club honors you have made the hand. The most you can lose is one spade trick and one club trick, as one spade goes away on the ♡A. Say the ♣10 loses to the ♣J and a spade comes back. Win the ♠A (or duck and win the spade return), cross to the ♣A and if the ♣K drops, the ♣Q is your eleventh trick. If not, discard the ♣Q on the ♡A and ruff a club. You still prevail when clubs are 3-3.

Given that West has the ♣K, this line only loses when East started with a singleton or doubleton jack. In other words, you have about a 90% chance of success. Incidentally, the best play for *two* tricks with this club layout, and no knowledge of the location of the opposing honors, is to plunk down the ♣A and then lead low to the ♣Q. If the ♣Q loses to the ♣K, enter your hand in some other suit and lead low to the ♣10. You wind up with at least two tricks unless West has specifically ♣Kx, about a 90% chance.

The West hand: ♠K J 6 ♡Q J 10 7 4 2 ◇J 5 ♣K 6
The East hand: ♠Q 9 5 3 ♡K 6 5 3 ◇4 ♣J 9 8 7

SOLUTION 48 (*ADVANCED*)

♠ A Q 3
♡ —
◇ 8 7 6 5 3 2
♣ 8 6 3 2

♠ K 10
♡ A K Q
◇ A Q J
♣ A K 10 9 7

You like your hand, in fact you love it, and open 2♣. Partner bids 2◇, waiting, and you bid 3♣, natural. Once partner supports clubs and later shows an ace, but denies the ♣Q in response to Keycard Blackwood, you have no qualms about bidding 6♣.

West leads the ♡10. You win, discarding a diamond from dummy, and plunk down the ♣A dropping the ♣Q from West. What now? Plan the play.

If you get the clubs right, you have no club loser and the most you can lose is one diamond. However, if you get the clubs wrong, will you be a dead duck if West has the ◇K? No. You will be alive and well *as long as you get the clubs wrong correctly!*

Cash two more hearts, discarding diamonds from dummy, and then three rounds of spades, discarding a diamond from your hand. With hearts and spades stripped, it is time to lead a trump from dummy. When East plays low, stick in the ♣10. If it wins, draw East's last trump, cross to dummy's ♣8 and try the diamond finesse for the overtrick. But what if the trump finesse loses? What if West was fooling you with ♣QJ doubleton? No problem, if the finesse loses, claim!

If West returns a diamond, it goes smack into your ◇AQ. If West returns a major suit, trump in dummy and discard the ◇Q from your hand. Had you plunked down the ♣K at Trick 3 thinking West might have ♣QJ doubleton, down you would go if West had the ◇K.

Consider this common card combination missing the jack and queen. Assume you have no information from the bidding and you cannot afford to lose a trick in the suit.

K 10 4 3 A 8 6 5 2

Start with the ace. If *East* follows with an honor, lead low to the ten. East is more likely to have a singleton honor than QJ doubleton.

The West hand: ♠ J 9 6 4 2 ♡ 10 9 8 4 2 ◇ K 4 ♣ Q
The East hand: ♠ 8 7 5 ♡ J 7 6 5 3 ◇ 10 9 ♣ J 5 4

PROBLEM 49 (*ADVANCED*)

♠ 9 6 3 2
♡ K 10 2
◇ A J 10 9 7
♣ 3

♠ A Q 7
♡ 3
◇ K Q 8 6 5 4
♣ A Q 2

With your side vulnerable, you open 1◇, West overcalls 1♡, and partner makes a negative double, unlimited, showing four spades. East ups the ante to 4♡, typically showing thirteen cards at this vulnerability. You double to show a strong hand lacking direction. Your double elicits 5◇ from partner, ending the auction. West leads the ♡Q. Plan the play. Diamonds are 1-1.

PROBLEM 50

♠ K 5 4 3
♡ A K J 6
◇ 7 5 2
♣ 10 4

♠ A J 10
♡ 7 2
◇ A K Q J 10 8
♣ J 9

Your accurate partnership bidding (bidding every suit in sight but clubs), has told the opponents that neither of you has a club stopper. Nevertheless, you do get to a neat 5◇ contract. Not being deaf, West leads the ♣A and then a club to East's ♣K. East exits with a diamond at Trick 3. Diamonds are 2-2. Plan the play.

PROBLEM 51

♠ Q 10 9 7 6
♡ K 5 2
◇ 7 5
♣ A 7 5

♠ A K J 5 4
♡ J 8 4 3
◇ A Q 6
♣ K

You open 1♠ and continue to game after partner gives you a limit raise. West leads the ♣J. Spades are 2-1. Plan the play.

PROBLEM 52 (*ADVANCED*)

♠ J 5 2
♡ J 10 9
◇ A 9 4 2
♣ Q 8 7

♠ 9 8 6
♡ A K Q 8 7
◇ 3
♣ A K 3 2

Partner raises your 1♡ opening to 2♡ and you bid 4♡. West leads the ♠A, ♠K and a third spade to East's ♠Q and East exits with the ◇K. Plan the play.

SOLUTION 49 (*ADVANCED*)

♠ 9 6 3 2
♡ K 10 2
◇ A J 10 9 7
♣ 3

♠ A Q 7
♡ 3
◇ K Q 8 6 5 4
♣ A Q 2

With your side vulnerable, you open 1◇, West overcalls 1♡, and partner makes a negative double, unlimited, showing four spades. East ups the ante to 4♡, typically showing thirteen cards at this vulnerability. You double to show a strong hand lacking direction. Your double elicits 5◇ from partner, ending the auction. West leads the ♡Q. Plan the play. Diamonds are 1-1.

You are looking at a heart loser along with two possible spade losers. The ♣Q is a mirage. The club finesse doesn't help even if it works. Nor does it help if West leads a club into your ♣AQ, as a spade discard from dummy does you no good. Concentrate on spades.

The sure way to avoid two spade losers, even if West has the ♠K, is to force West to lead a spade into your ♠AQ. You can do it, but it requires a little work!

Your first important play comes at Trick 1 where you must duck the opening lead to keep East, the danger hand, from getting in to lead a spade. Say West shifts to a safe trump (best) at Trick 2. Win in dummy, play the ♣A and ruff a club and now another big play, the ♡K. Assuming East covers, ruff, then ruff your ♣Q eliminating that suit, and exit dummy with the ♡10, discarding a spade as West surely has the ♡J.

What is West to lead? A spade return goes smack into 'Jaws' (the ♠AQ), and any other return allows you to ruff in dummy and discard the ♠Q from your hand.

Would you like to know what you have done on this hand in 'bridgese'? You have made an avoidance ducking play at Trick 1, then you transferred the heart menace from East to West, and for kickers you made a loser-on-loser throw-in play after stripping the hand. This is an advanced hand, after all, but the key, as ever, is first recognizing the problem and then figuring out how to resolve it.

The West hand: ♠ K 5 4 ♡ Q J 9 8 6 ◇ 3 ♣ K J 6 4
The East hand: ♠ J 10 8 ♡ A 7 5 4 ◇ 2 ♣ 10 9 8 7 5

SOLUTION 50

♠ K 5 4 3
♡ A K J 6
♢ 7 5 2
♣ 10 4

♠ A J 10
♡ 7 2
♢ A K Q J 10 8
♣ J 9

Your accurate partnership bidding (bidding every suit in sight but clubs), has told the opponents that neither of you has a club stopper. Nevertheless, you do get to a neat 5♢ contract. Not being deaf, West leads the ♣A and then a club to East's ♣K. East exits with a diamond at Trick 3. Diamonds are 2-2. Plan the play.

You have ten top tricks and would like to combine your chances in the majors to secure that extra needed trick. These are your 'combining options' after drawing trumps:

1. Play the ♠AK and if the ♠Q doesn't drop (it will about 20% of the time), take the heart finesse.
2. Play the ♡AK and trump a heart. If the queen doesn't drop (it will about 37% of the time), take the spade finesse in one direction or the other. Just get it right!

The winner is (2) because it is more likely that the ♡Q will show up after you trump a heart than the ♠Q will show up after you cash the ♠AK. In addition, if you trump a heart and no ♡Q appears, you have the option of taking the spade finesse *in either direction*, always a plus.

The West hand: ♠Q 6 2 ♡9 8 4 3 ♢4 3 ♣A Q 8 6.
The East hand: ♠9 8 7 ♡Q 10 5 ♢9 6 ♣K 7 5 3 2

Notice the opening lead was from the ♣AQ. When you know partner has the ♣K (they knew it in Outer Mongolia), it's not a very risky lead at all, is it?

Also, if the ♡Q doesn't fall and it comes to playing spades, the idea is to play the hand that started with more spades for the ♠Q. If you can't tell, start with the ♠J hoping to coax a cover. If no cover is forthcoming, you are on your own. However, if you know that West adores covering honors, you have a pretty good idea who has the ♠Q.

SOLUTION 51

♠ Q 10 9 7 6
♡ K 5 2
♢ 7 5
♣ A 7 5

♠ A K J 5 4
♡ J 8 4 3
♢ A Q 6
♣ K

You open 1♠ and continue to game after partner gives you a limit raise. West leads the ♣J. Spades are 2-1. Plan the play.

This hand, a mate to Problem 11, is another finessaholic's dream. There are three, count 'em, three finesses available.

1. Leading up to the ♡K.
2. Leading up to the ♡J if the ♡K loses to the ♡A.
3. The diamond finesse.

If any one of these three works (87%) you make 4♠. Are you satisfied?

You shouldn't be. There is a 100% play.

Win the ♣K, draw trumps ending in dummy, discard a diamond on the ♣A, ruff a club, stripping that suit, and exit with the ♢A and ♢Q! Yes, you read correctly.

It doesn't matter who wins the trick, once either opponent leads a heart you can lose no more than two heart tricks. If the opponents opt not to lead a heart, but instead present you with a ruff and sluff, ruff in your hand, the *longer* heart hand, and discard a heart from dummy, the *shorter* heart hand. That's the way to handle a ruff and sluff.

Card combinations that feature a king or a queen facing a jack lend themselves to throw-ins. If you can draw trumps leaving trumps in both hands, strip any side suit (here, clubs), and use an *equal*-length side suit (here, diamonds) as your throw-in suit, you are in great shape. The ♢Q is an optical illusion. Let's hope you weren't sucked in by it — again!

The West hand: ♠3 ♡Q 9 7 ♢K 8 4 3 2 ♣J 10 8 4
The East hand: ♠8 2 ♡A 10 6 ♢J 10 9 ♣Q 9 6 3 2

SOLUTION 52 (*ADVANCED*)

♠ J 5 2
♡ J 10 9
◇ A 9 4 2
♣ Q 8 7

♠ 9 8 6
♡ A K Q 8 7
◇ 3
♣ A K 3 2

Partner raises your 1♡ opening to 2♡ and you bid 4♡. West leads the ♠A, ♠K and a third spade to East's ♠Q and East exits with the ◇K. Plan the play.

There are two possible lines of play both aimed at dealing with that &%$# fourth club.

Line #1: Draw two rounds of trumps and play three high clubs. If clubs break 3-3, draw the remaining trumps and claim. If someone ruffs the third club you are down, but at least you can ruff your fourth club in dummy and break even. This play gains when the player with three (or four) trumps has four clubs allowing you to trump a club in dummy. It is clearly a better line than just drawing trumps, hoping clubs are 3-3, and folding up your tent when they are 4-2. However, the player with the longer trump holding usually also has the shorter club holding.

Line #2: The line that works whenever trumps are 3-2 is better. Win the ◇A, trump a diamond high, cross to the ♡9 and trump another diamond high. You still have the ♡A8 while dummy has the ♡J10. Enter dummy with the ♣Q and trump dummy's last diamond with the ♡A, cross to the ♡10 and discard that fourth club on the ♡J, drawing the last trump at the same time. The ♣AK will be your last two tricks. You didn't have to trump that fourth club, you discarded it on a trump!

Think about this: When you have a solid 5-3 trump fit, and you trump a loser in the shorter trump hand, you score six trump tricks. In order to score six trump tricks by trumping in your hand, the longer trump hand, you have to trump *three* times, reducing your trump length to two while dummy has three. The next step is to draw three rounds of trumps. This allows you to discard a loser from your hand on the third trump. It's called a *dummy reversal.* Make sure you have enough dummy entries before you try to pull off one of these.

And, yes, if East had returned a trump rather than the tempting diamond from the ◇KQJ, the dummy reversal would have failed due to dummy entry shortage problems.

The West hand: ♠A K 4 ♡6 3 2 ◇10 8 7 6 5 ♣9 4
The East hand: ♠Q 10 7 3 ♡5 4 ◇K Q J ♣J 10 6 5

PROBLEM 53

♠ Q 9 5 4 2
♡ A 3 2
◇ A 3 2
♣ K 4

♠ A K 10 8 6
♡ K J 10
◇ K J 7
♣ A J

After you open 2NT (yes, 2NT with five spades), partner surprises you by bidding 3♡, a transfer to spades! You jump accept by bidding 4♠, showing a great hand for spades with at least four spades. Partner bids 6♠. West leads the ♣10. Plan the play.

PROBLEM 54

♠ J 10 9 7
♡ J 10 7
◇ 9 5
♣ A 10 6 2

♠ A Q 8 5 2
♡ A K 5
◇ A K
♣ K 5 3

After opening 2♣, strong and artificial, you wind up in the 'somewhat' pushy contract of 6♠. The opening lead is the ◇J. Think positively and give yourself the best chance. Trumps are not 4-0. Plan the play.

PROBLEM 55

♠ K 8 6 5
♡ J 7
◇ A K 10
♣ A Q 9 7

♠ Q 7 3 2
♡ 5 3 2
◇ 8 4 2
♣ K J 10

West opens 1♡, partner doubles, East raises to 2♡, and you try 2♠. Partner, who can never take a joke, raises to 4♠. West leads the ♡K, continues with the ♡Q, East playing high-low (attitude), and plays a third heart to East's ♡A, which you ruff. What now?

PROBLEM 56

♠ J 10
♡ A 10 8 2
◇ A K 4
♣ 10 7 6 2

♠ A Q
♡ K Q J 9 7 6 4
◇ 8 5
♣ A Q

You wind up in 6♡ after partner opens 1♣, supports your hearts, and shows two aces and the ◇K in response to your Keycard Blackwood inquiries. West leads the ◇J. Hearts are 1-1. Plan the play.

SOLUTION 53

♠ Q 9 5 4 2
♡ A 3 2
◇ A 3 2
♣ K 4

♠ A K 10 8 6
♡ K J 10
◇ K J 7
♣ A J

After you open 2NT (yes, 2NT with five spades), partner surprises you by bidding 3♡, a transfer to spades! You jump accept by bidding 4♠, showing a great hand for spades with at least four spades. Partner bids 6♠. West leads the ♣10. Plan the play.

You have possible losers in two suits, both equally divided, both missing the queen. A finessaholic draws trumps, strips clubs, and takes two red-suit finesses. He will be victorious 75% of the time; that's how often one expects to win at least one of two finesses. Not bad, but terrible on this hand.

A stronger player draws trumps, strips clubs, and plays the ace, king and jack of *diamonds*, forcing a *heart* return. Once either opponent leads a heart there is no longer a guess in that suit and the slam can be chalked up.

Notice if you play the ♡A, ♡K and ♡J, conceding a heart trick and forcing a diamond return, you could go down. East may win and lead a diamond and West may have the queen.

The West hand: ♠7 ♡9 8 4 ◇Q 10 8 6 ♣10 9 8 5 2
The East hand: ♠J 3 ♡Q 7 6 5 ◇9 5 4 ♣Q 7 6 3

Tip

When you have two equally-divided suits and either can be used as your throw-in suit to force a lead in the other, ask yourself which suit you most want led to you. Once decided, use the other as your throw-in suit.

Tip

When you have a five-card major with a balanced hand and 20-21 HCP, you are usually better placed opening 2NT than the major. If you open your major, partner's 1NT response often gets 3NT played from the wrong side. Many top players open 2NT with 19 HCP and a strong five-card suit, easily the equivalent of 20 HCP.

SOLUTION 54

♠ J 10 9 7
♡ J 10 7
◇ 9 5
♣ A 10 6 2

♠ A Q 8 5 2
♡ A K 5
◇ A K
♣ K 5 3

After opening 2♣, strong and artificial, you wind up in the 'somewhat' pushy contract of 6♠. The opening lead is the ◇J. Think positively and give yourself the best chance. Trumps are not 4-0. Plan the play.

Unless you get a miracle in both clubs and hearts, you have *at least* one loser between those two suits. Bottom line is that you need to find the ♠K with East, so assume it's there. But you still have to deal with hearts and clubs.

Cash a second diamond, stripping that suit, cross to the ♣A and run the ♠J. Say it wins, so you run the ♠10 and draw trumps. Let's assume trumps were 3-1, West discarding a couple of diamonds. You are still alive! Cash the ♡A, the ♣K, and lead a third club toward the ♣10-6 in dummy. Keep in mind you still have a spade entry to dummy for the heart finesse if needed.

What do you need? You need to find clubs 3-3 or East having a doubleton honor. If so, when you lead up to the ♣10, West will, perforce, take the trick with the other club honor and the ♣10 will provide a resting place for your losing heart. If clubs do not come in, cross to dummy with a trump and take the heart finesse.

Notice that you worked with the longer side suit, clubs, before hearts. *Equally-divided side suits are the pits.* However, sometimes they can be your throw-in suit to force a lead in a suit you would rather not lead yourself. Not the case here.

Tip:

The best play for three club tricks given a side-suit entry to dummy, is ♣A, ♣K and low to the ♣10, playing for East to have honor doubleton or the suit to break 3-3. However, with hand entries to burn, cash the ♣K and then lead low to the ♣A. West may have QJxx(x) and play an honor fearing you are about to play the ♣10. Now, after you take the ♣A, return to your hand and lead up to the ♣10, ending up with three club tricks.

The West hand: ♠6 ♡Q 8 4 3 ◇J 10 8 2 ♣Q 9 7 4
The East hand: ♠K 4 3 ♡9 6 2 ◇Q 7 6 4 3 ♣J 8

SOLUTION 55

♠ K 8 6 5
♡ J 7
◇ A K 10
♣ A Q 9 7

♠ Q 7 3 2
♡ 5 3 2
◇ 8 4 2
♣ K J 10

West opens 1♡, partner doubles, East raises to 2♡, and you try 2♠. Partner, who can never take a joke, raises to 4♠. West leads the ♡K, continues with the ♡Q, East playing high-low (attitude), and plays a third heart to East's ♡A, which you ruff. What now?

You have already lost two heart tricks but with a little luck you'll be able to dispose of your diamond loser on a club. The problem is the trump suit. You have to hold your trump losses to one trick and there are only two holdings that allow for this. You have to find one opponent with ♠Ax. If East has ♠Ax, you must lead a low spade to your ♠Q and then duck a spade to East's now lone ♠A. However, if West has ♠Ax, you must lead a low spade from your hand to the ♠K and then duck a spade to West's now lone ♠A.

As West opened the bidding and East has already turned up with the ♡A, West must have the ♠A. Backing your judgment, cross to a club and lead a low spade to the ♠K. Assuming it wins, duck a second spade and hope to see the ♠A come tumbling down on your left. Guess what? You have just made a *finesse obbligato*, an obligatory finesse, and it worked!

Tip:
As a defender holding QJx(x)(x) of a side suit that you haven't led, when you see the AK10 to your left in dummy, it is usually safe to switch to a ***low*** *card in that suit early in the hand. It is unlikely that declarer, unless desperate, will insert the ten. Just play it cool.*

The West hand: ♠A 9 ♡K Q 10 8 4 ◇Q J 6 3 ♣3 2
The East hand: ♠J 10 4 ♡A 9 6 ◇9 7 5 ♣8 6 5 4

SOLUTION 56

♠ J 10
♡ A 10 8 2
♢ A K 4
♣ 10 7 6 2

♠ A Q
♡ K Q J 9 7 6 4
♢ 8 5
♣ A Q

You wind up in 6♡ after partner opens 1♣, supports your hearts, and shows two aces and the ♢K in response to your Keycard Blackwood inquiries. West leads the ♢J. Hearts are 1-1. Plan the play.

You have two suits that include finesses for a king. However, one suit is longer, clubs, a suit that offers additional chances if the finesse loses because of the presence of the ♣10.

Win the diamond lead, cross to your hand with a heart, strip the diamonds, enter dummy with a heart and lead a club to the ♣Q. Assuming the finesse loses, West's only safe return is a club, so assume a club is returned to your ♣A. (Some Wests may not be that clever and that is why it is a good idea to strip side suits from both your hand and dummy early on. Now if an opponent leads a 'stripped' suit, it usually costs the defending side a trick.)

In any case, win the ♣A, cross to dummy with a trump and ruff a club. If the ♣J appears, the ♣10 in dummy means you won't need the spade finesse. If the ♣J doesn't appear, take the spade finesse. After clubs are played three times the ♣J will show up about 37% of the time. Not a bad way to stay alive before taking the spade finesse.

The West hand: ♠K 8 6 5 ♡5 ♢J 10 9 3 2 ♣K J 4
The East hand: ♠9 7 4 3 2 ♡3 ♢Q 7 6 ♣9 8 5 3

Dummy		You
♣ Jxxx		♣ K

Say this is your club side suit in a trump contract. Start by leading a low club from dummy, hoping to steal a trick with the ♣K. If that doesn't work, don't give up. Assuming you have enough dummy entries, trump two clubs. On a good day you will trump out the ♣Q and the ♣J will be high. Play the same way if your singleton is the ♣Q. The ♣Q loses to one honor, but the other honor may drop after you ruff two of dummy's small cards. P.S. You need plenty of dummy entries to try this.

PROBLEM 57

♠ K 9 3
♡ K Q 9 6 2
♢ K 10 4 3
♣ 6

♠ A Q 10 2
♡ J 10
♢ A Q 9
♣ K J 5 2

You open 1NT, partner transfers you to 2♡ and then bids 3♢, natural and forcing. With a doubleton heart and most of your strength in the blacks you try 3NT, the final contract. West leads the ♣7, East playing the ♣3. You win the ♣J. Now what?

PROBLEM 58

♠ A 7 3
♡ 9 8
♢ A Q 9 7 6
♣ K 8 5

♠ K J 10 6 5 2
♡ A J
♢ K J 3
♣ 6 4

You open 1♠, partner responds 2♢, East bids 2♡, you repeat your spades and partner bids 4♠. Simple enough. West leads the ♡3, fetching the ♡K from East. Plan the play.

PROBLEM 59 (*ADVANCED*)

♠ 9 6 5
♡ A K 2
◇ 8 4 3
♣ A J 9 8

♠ A K Q J 10 4
♡ Q 3
◇ K 7 6
♣ Q 10

After partner opens 1♣, you cough and splutter your way into a contract of 5♠, a contract that gives you the same feeling as kissing your sister; playing 5NT is even worse. West leads the ♡10. Plan the play.

PROBLEM 60

♠ J 5
♡ A 6 2
◇ A K 10 4
♣ 7 5 3 2

♠ A K 4 3
♡ K Q 4
◇ Q J 3
♣ A K J

After you open 2♣ and rebid 2NT over partner's unlimited 2◇ response, partner saves time and raises to 6NT. There figures to be at least 34 HCP between the two hands, usually enough. The opening lead is the ♡J. Plan the play.

SOLUTION 57

♠ K 9 3
♡ K Q 9 6 2
◇ K 10 4 3
♣ 6

♠ A Q 10 2
♡ J 10
◇ A Q 9
♣ K J 5 2

You open 1NT, partner transfers you to 2♡ and then bids 3◇, natural and forcing. With a doubleton heart and most of your strength in the blacks you try 3NT, the final contract. West leads the ♣7, East playing the ♣3. You win the ♣J. Now what?

You start with seven top tricks and have chances for extra tricks in three suits. Hearts offers the chance for the most tricks, but runs the risk of East having the ♡A and pounding a likely ♣9 through your ♣K. It appears from the lead and the carding that East has the ♣983. If this happens, you will not be a happy camper. Surely you can do better than putting your contract up for grabs at Trick 2!

Might as well see if the diamonds or spades come in for four tricks each. If so, you won't need to risk your contract by leading a heart. You will have taken the first nine tricks.

Proper technique when playing spades is the ♠Q, then over to the ♠K and back to the ♠A. This allows you to finesse the ♠10 if West shows out on the second spade. In diamonds, proper technique is the ◇Q, then the ◇A, and finally over to the ◇K. This allows you to finesse the ◇10 if East shows out on the second diamond. Leading the queen rather than the ace in each suit first gives you a better chance of getting a count card from the opponents. Each opponent may think partner has the ace.

As the cards lie, you take four tricks in each suit and wind up taking the first nine tricks. If you strike out in either one or both of the suits you tested, you will be forced to lead a heart. But guess what? You still make your contract if West has the ♡A. What can West do? West does best to duck the first heart and win the second, but has to concede a ninth trick to your ♣K.

The West hand: ♠J 5 4 ♡5 4 ◇8 7 6 ♣A Q 10 7 4
The East hand: ♠8 7 6 ♡A 8 7 3 ◇J 5 2 ♣9 8 3

SOLUTION 58

♠ A 7 3
♡ 9 8
◇ A Q 9 7 6
♣ K 8 5

♠ K J 10 6 5 2
♡ A J
◇ K J 3
♣ 6 4

You open 1♠, partner responds 2◇, East bids 2♡, you repeat your spades and partner bids 4♠. Simple enough. West leads the ♡3, fetching the ♡K from East. Plan the play.

You have a heart loser, two possible club losers and a possible spade loser. On the plus side you have a side suit that can furnish discards for two of your losers providing you resolve your trump problem. What is important to realize is that West is the danger hand, the hand that can lead a club through dummy's ♣K.

You have to think differently when there is a danger hand. You have to think *avoidance*. You have to direct your finesses into the non-danger hand, East. Furthermore, if you win the ♡A, and East gets in, East can put West in with the ♡Q, defeating your plan. Therefore, the first obligatory play is to duck the ♡K and win the likely heart return.

Now is the time to attack the trump suit, making sure West does not get in. Lead the ♠K and then the ♠J. If West follows low, play low — perhaps losing to ♠Qx in the East hand. No matter. You have ensured the contract. If East has the ♣A and doesn't cash it, he goes to bed with it. If the ♠J holds, you have the rest of the tricks. If West shows out on the second spade, play the ♠A and concede a spade to East, who again must cash the ♣A or lose it.

Bravo, you have made an 'avoidance duck' at Trick 1 plus an avoidance finesse at Trick 4!

Tip:

Protecting an unguarded king from a premature attack is often the overriding consideration when planning the play.

The West hand: ♠Q 9 8 ♡Q 7 3 ◇8 4 2 ♣J 9 7 3
The East hand: ♠4 ♡K 10 6 5 4 2 ◇10 5 ♣A Q 10 2

SOLUTION 59 (ADVANCED)

♠ 9 6 5
♡ A K 2
◇ 8 4 3
♣ A J 9 8

♠ A K Q J 10 4
♡ Q 3
◇ K 7 6
♣ Q 10

After partner opens 1♣, you cough and splutter your way into a contract of 5♠, a contract that gives you the same feeling as kissing your sister; playing 5NT is even worse. West leads the ♡10. Plan the play.

The idea is to keep East from getting in for fear of a diamond switch through the ◇K. East is the danger hand. Unfortunately, the club finesse is headed smack into East — or is it?

Win the ♡Q and play the ♠AK. If spades are 2-2, you have a claimer. Play the ♡A and ♡K discarding a club and then the ♣A and ♣J, discarding a diamond if East plays low. Say West wins the ♣K. If West doesn't lead a diamond, you have the rest, discarding two more diamonds on winning clubs.

If spades are 3-1, leave a spade at large and play the ♡AK discarding a *club*, followed by the ♣A and ♣J discarding a diamond if East plays low. If West wins and clubs are 4-3, the most the opponents can take is the ◇A as there are two good clubs in dummy for diamond discards, with the ♠9 as the entry to dummy. If West started with five clubs and East has the remaining trump, and West is smart enough to lead a club, East ruffs, you overruff, cross to dummy with a trump, discard a diamond on a winning club and lead up to the ◇K. Cheer up. This is unlikely to happen — besides, East may have the ◇A.

If the ♣J holds, try the ♣9. If East covers, ruff high, enter dummy with the ♠9 and discard a second diamond on a high club. However, if East has five clubs and ducks twice, and West has the remaining trump, West will trump but is now endplayed. A heart exit is a ruff and sluff and a diamond lead goes to your ◇K.

Tip:
*With a solid trump suit including a low trump, be **very** reluctant to give up that low trump. It often can be used to get to dummy.*

The West hand: ♠ 7 3 ♡ 10 9 8 5 ◇ A Q 2 ♣ 7 5 3 2
The East hand: ♠ 8 2 ♡ J 7 6 4 ◇ J 10 9 5 ♣ K 6 4

SOLUTION 60

♠ J 5
♡ A 6 2
◇ A K 10 4
♣ 7 5 3 2

♠ A K 4 3
♡ K Q 4
◇ Q J 3
♣ A K J

After you open 2♣ and rebid 2NT over partner's unlimited 2◇ response, partner saves time and raises to 6NT. There figures to be at least 34 HCP between the two hands, usually enough. The opening lead is the ♡J. Plan the play.

You are looking pretty good with eleven top tricks and chances in the black suits for an extra trick or even two. What exactly are those chances?

1. Cash the ♣A, cross to the ◇A and then take the club finesse. If that wins you have twelve tricks. If it doesn't, you still survive if clubs are 3-3. That logs in at about 68%: either the finesse works or a 3-3 break if it doesn't. And let's toss in the singleton ♠Q, a robust extra 1%.
2. Lead a spade to the ♠J. If West has the ♠Q, you have twelve tricks. If East has the ♠Q, cash the ♣A, cross to the ◇A and then take the club finesse. This line, needing one of two finesses or the ♣Q singleton, logs in at a bit over 75%. Go for Line #2.

Bottom line: One of two finesses offers a better chance than a finesse or a 3-3 break.

The West hand: ♠Q 8 ♡J 10 9 7 ◇9 8 6 ♣Q 10 6 4
The East hand: ♠10 9 7 6 2 ♡8 5 3 ◇7 5 2 ♣9 8

PROBLEM 61 (*ADVANCED*)

♠ Q
♡ J 8 4 3
◇ A 5 4
♣ A Q J 6 5

♠ A J 9 6 5
♡ A K
◇ Q 2
♣ 10 9 8 3

Here's your chance to match wits with many-time World Champion Bob Hamman. Bob played this hand in 3NT at the 2008 Boston National Championships (IMP scoring).

North opened 1◇ (1♣ would have been strong and artificial), Bob bid 1♠ and then 3NT after partner rebid 2♣. West led the ♡10, East encouraging. Plan the play.

PROBLEM 62

♠ 5
♡ K J 4
◇ A Q 10 8 5 2
♣ A 5 4

♠ K Q 9
♡ A 5 3 2
◇ K 9
♣ Q J 10 9

You open 1NT and land in 3NT, refusing partner's slam try in diamonds. West leads the ♠7, East plays the ♠J. Plan the play.

PROBLEM 63

♠ 7 5 2
♡ J 9
♢ A Q J 10 2
♣ Q J 2

♠ A 8 4
♡ A K Q
♢ 9 7 3
♣ A 10 9 4

East opens 1♠, you overcall 1NT and partner bids 3NT. West leads the ♠9, overtaken by the ♠10 that you allow to hold. East continues with the ♠K. Plan the play.

PROBLEM 64

♠ A 8 3 2
♡ 8 7 5
♢ 9 7
♣ A K J 10

♠ K Q J 10 7 6 5
♡ A 10 9
♢ A 10
♣ 3

After partner opens 1♣ and supports spades, wild horses can't keep you out of 6♠. West leads the ♡K, East plays the ♡2. Plan the play.

SOLUTION 61 (*ADVANCED*)

♠ Q
♡ J 8 4 3
◇ A 5 4
♣ A Q J 6 5

♠ A J 9 6 5
♡ A K
◇ Q 2
♣ 10 9 8 3

Here's your chance to match wits with many-time World Champion Bob Hamman. Bob played this hand in 3NT at the 2008 Boston National Championships (IMP scoring). North opened 1◇ (1♣ would have been strong and artificial), Bob bid 1♠ and then 3NT after partner rebid 2♣. West led the ♡10, East encouraging. Plan the play.

Things look pretty good; 6♣ doesn't look too bad either, but you are in 3NT.

Bob wasn't worried about hearts, it was his diamond stopper that bothered him. He didn't like the idea of East getting in early and shifting to a diamond, West having the ◇K. This is how experts think when in a good contract like this one. What can go wrong? And then try to avoid that happening. When in a desperate contract, the more usual scenario, the operative question is: What can go right — and then play for it!

Hamman took the ♡K at Trick 1 and noticed that if the club finesse lost to East, he would only have eight tricks. Furthermore, if a diamond came back and West had both missing kings he would be in big trouble.

Our hero decided it was time to make a newspaper column play. He led the ♣10 to the *ace* and ran the ♠Q into West, the non-danger hand. If the ♠Q had held or it had been covered, Bob would have reverted to clubs and taken nine tricks: four clubs, two spades, two hearts and a diamond. As it happened, West won the ♠K and exited a low heart to Bob's ♡A. Bob cashed his two high spades, no ♠10 appearing, and continued with the ♣9, driving out East's ♣K. East shifted to the ◇J, but it was too late. The ◇Q was covered with the ◇K and taken by dummy's ◇A. Bob wound up with four clubs, two spades, two hearts and a diamond, not having to deal with a diamond lead through his ◇Q until he had nine tricks.

The key play was crossing to the ♣A at Trick 2, knowing that even if West had the ♠K, the ◇Q would be safe from attack and there would still be time to develop spade tricks.

The West hand: ♠K 10 8 4 3 ♡10 5 ◇K 8 7 6 ♣7 2
The East hand: ♠7 2 ♡Q 9 7 6 2 ◇J 10 9 3 ♣K 4

SOLUTION 62

♠ 5
♡ K J 4
◇ A Q 10 8 5 2
♣ A 5 4

♠ K Q 9
♡ A 5 3 2
◇ K 9
♣ Q J 10 9

You open 1NT and land in 3NT, refusing partner's slam try in diamonds. West leads the ♠7, East plays the ♠J. Plan the play.

For starters, take the trick. There is no point in ducking. Also, take the trick with the king, keeping West in the dark, at least temporarily, as to who has the ♠Q. You have seven top tricks with extra tricks possibly available in three suits. Diamonds is your best suit and on a good day the suit will divide 3-2 or the ◇J will be singleton (70+%) and you will roll home with at least ten tricks. But what if diamonds are 4-1 (28%)? If West has four diamonds to the ◇J, it is safe to lose a diamond to West as West cannot attack your ♠Q. You wind up with at least nine tricks: five diamonds, two hearts, a club and a spade.

But what if East has four diamonds to the ◇J? You can't give up a diamond to East for fear of a spade lead through your ♠Q9 as West is marked with the ♠A10, so you must look elsewhere. Your best bet is the club finesse. If that works, you get at least three clubs tricks to go along with three diamonds, two hearts and a spade. But the club finesse goes smack into East as does the heart finesse.

The simple solution is to cross to the ♡K and lead a diamond to the *nine*. If it wins, you have six diamond tricks; if it loses to West you have five diamond tricks, a safe five diamond tricks. Say West wins and leads a club. Win the ♣A and play the ◇A, killing your ◇K but liberating the suit for five tricks, all you need for your contract.

Sometimes you have to make a safety play in a strong suit, perhaps conceding a trick that may not have to be lost, to keep the danger hand off lead — something to consider when things look too good! Safety plays like this are anathema to matchpoint players who live and die for overtricks. They wouldn't be caught dead leading a diamond to the ◇9, far and away the proper play at IMP scoring.

The West hand: ♠A 10 8 7 2 ♡10 7 6 ◇6 ♣8 7 3 2
The East hand: ♠J 6 4 3 ♡Q 9 8 ◇J 7 4 3 ♣K 6

SOLUTION 63

♠ 7 5 2
♡ J 9
◊ A Q J 10 2
♣ Q J 2

♠ A 8 4
♡ A K Q
◊ 9 7 3
♣ A 10 9 4

East opens 1♠, you overcall 1NT and partner bids 3NT. West leads the ♠9, overtaken by the ♠10 that you allow to hold. East continues with the ♠K. Plan the play.

Most players would automatically hold up until the third round of spades, but the rule is this: take the ace when it exhausts the player with the shorter holding in the suit. Since East started with at least five spades, it is safe to win the second spade.

Back to basics: You start with six sure tricks and can make four extra tricks if the diamond finesse works, three extra if the club finesse works. Therefore, if either finesse works you will make your contract. However, you *know* that the club finesse will work and the diamond finesse won't. How do you know?

Count points! Add your HCP to dummy's *before* playing to the first trick — not to see if partner has bid correctly, but rather to see how many HCP the opponents have. Here you have 28 HCP between the hands leaving the bad guys with 12 HCP. Since East has opened the bidding, East figures to have all 12 points. Translation: East has both minor-suit kings. Also, if you wish to see a really forlorn face, glance over at West, a player who does not have a single high card point!

Cross to the ◊A and run the ♣Q. Unless East has psyched an opening bid, the club finesse will work and you will make nine tricks. In addition, if the ◊K happens to fall singleton, you will take the rest of the tricks — yet another reason for winning the second spade — actually a good case could be made for winning the first spade given the bidding. It is certainly the right play at matchpoints as you have a chance to take all thirteen tricks with virtually no risk.

Tip:
Use the bidding to guide you in the play. Make a habit of adding your HCP to dummy's not only to determine how many HCP they have, but also the likely location of those points.

The West hand: ♠9 6 ♡8 7 6 4 3 2 ◊8 6 4 ♣5 3
The East hand: ♠K Q J 10 3 ♡10 5 ◊K 5 ♣K 8 7 6

SOLUTION 64

♠ A 8 3 2
♡ 8 7 5
◇ 9 7
♣ A K J 10

♠ K Q J 10 7 6 5
♡ A 10 9
◇ A 10
♣ 3

After partner opens 1♣ and supports spades, wild horses can't keep you out of 6♠. West leads the ♡K, East plays the ♡2. Plan the play.

With three red-suit losers staring you in the face, two of them immediate losers in hearts, you must do something with those clubs after drawing trumps. There is the straight club finesse. If that works (50%) you are home. But why toy with a 50% play when a 100% play is staring you in the face?

Play the ♣A and ♣K discarding a heart and lead the ♣J. If East plays low, discard a second heart. Assuming West wins, it's all over but the claiming. You will ruff West's heart exit, cross to dummy with a trump and discard your losing diamond on the ♣10. If East has the ♣Q, the ♣J will win as you discard a second heart and all you will lose is a diamond. In this case a ruffing finesse (what you did in clubs) is far safer than a simple finesse because it allows you to get rid of immediate losers quicker and with complete safety.

As an aside, if dummy's clubs were ♣AKJx, you should lead a club to the ♣J, playing West for the ♣Q. The 50% finesse is better than playing the ♣A and ♣K and trumping a club hoping the ♣Q makes an appearance. With only five clubs between your hand and dummy, your chance of dropping the ♣Q in three rounds isn't even half as good as the finesse. The ♣10 makes all the difference in the world.

The West hand: ♠9 ♡K Q J 4 ◇Q 8 6 3 ♣8 6 5 4
The East hand: ♠4 ♡6 3 2 ◇K J 5 4 2 ♣Q 9 7 2

PROBLEM 65

♠ A 6 4 3
♡ 10 2
◇ K 9 2
♣ Q J 6 5

♠ J 7 5
♡ A Q 5
◇ A J 4
♣ A K 8 2

You open 1♣ and rebid 2NT after partner responds 1♠. Partner raises to 3NT.

Undeterred by the 1♠ response, West leads the ♠2. You play low from dummy, East wins the ♠K and returns the ♠8 to your ♠J and West's ♠Q as you play low again. West stubbornly continues with the ♠10, East discarding the ♡6. Plan the play from here (neither player is void in clubs).

PROBLEM 66 (*ADVANCED*)

♠ 7 5 3
♡ Q 10 8
◇ A 6 5
♣ A K 4 3

♠ A Q
♡ A K J 9 7 4 3 2
◇ —
♣ J 6 2

After partner opens 1♣ and eventually supports hearts, serious control-bidding follows, and rather than settle for a somewhat conservative contract of 6♡, you shoot the moon and bid 7♡! West leads the ◇Q. Plan the play.

PROBLEM 67

♠ A
♡ A 6 5
◇ K 8 6 5 4 2
♣ 8 7 6

♠ K Q 3 2
♡ K J 4 2
◇ 9 3
♣ A K 5

A quick 1NT-3NT sequence ends with the ♠J lead from West. Plan the play.

PROBLEM 68 (*ADVANCED*)

♠ 3
♡ K 7 4 2
◇ Q 10 7 6
♣ A K Q 2

♠ A J 8
♡ A Q 6
◇ K J 9 8
♣ 10 6 5

After you open 1NT, partner bids 2♣ and you wind up in 3NT. You notice that 6◇ would have been a nice contract, but difficult to reach. West leads the ♠4 against your 3NT contract, East playing the ♠K. Plan the play in 3NT and forget 6◇! The literature is filled with stories of declarers who started to play the hand in the contract they wanted to be in rather than the one they were in!

SOLUTION 65

♠ A 6 4 3
♡ 10 2
◇ K 9 2
♣ Q J 6 5

♠ J 7 5
♡ A Q 5
◇ A J 4
♣ A K 8 2

You open 1♣ and rebid 2NT after partner responds 1♠. Partner raises to 3NT. Undeterred, West leads the ♠2. You play low from dummy, East wins the ♠K and returns the ♠8 to your ♠J and West's ♠Q. West stubbornly continues with the ♠10, East discarding the ♡6. Plan the play from here (neither is void in clubs).

Definitely win the ♠A. No point in holding up a third time and there is a very good reason not to. Patience. You have eight top tricks plus two possible finesses for a ninth. One of two finesses is 75%, but by now we know that 75% does not compare to 100%.

In order to prepare for a throw-in play (the way to avoid a finesse), start with four rounds of clubs ending in dummy, and exit dummy with a spade to West's ♠9, discarding a heart. West must lead a red card, conceding a ninth trick. After West leads one red suit, take a finesse in the other red suit, playing for a safe overtrick.

The West hand: ♠Q 10 9 2 ♡K 4 ◇Q 7 6 ♣10 9 7 3
The East hand: ♠K 8 ♡J 9 8 7 6 3 ◇10 8 5 3 ♣4

This hand reinforces a common theme: it is far safer to make a throw-in play to force a favorable lead than to attack the suit yourself. The secret is to strip *all* safe exit cards from the hand that you are throwing in and politely wait for your gift return. Notice West's lead: the ♠2 from ♠Q1092. When an opponent has bid the suit, it is better to lead low in case partner has an honor doubleton.

Tip:

*When defending a notrump contract, lead low from three-card honor sequences in a **bid** suit, catering to partner having an honor doubleton, when holding an outside entry. At IMP scoring where overtricks are not a major concern, but defeating the contract is, it is actually wiser to lead low from the QJ10xx or even KQJxx. If it doesn't work, don't call me, and don't write. However, from the QJ108x or the KQJ9x, lead a top honor regardless.*

SOLUTION 66 (*ADVANCED*)

♠ 7 5 3
♡ Q 10 8
◇ A 6 5
♣ A K 4 3

♠ A Q
♡ A K J 9 7 4 3 2
◇ —
♣ J 6 2

After partner opens 1♣ and eventually supports hearts, serious control-bidding follows, and rather than settle for a somewhat conservative contract of 6♡, you shoot the moon and bid 7♡! West leads the ◇Q: Plan the play.

With twelve top tricks, the idea is to work with the clubs, trying to avoid the spade finesse. It might look right to discard a club on the ◇A and then try to set up the clubs with a ruff hoping the suit breaks 3-3. If it doesn't, take the spade finesse.

It might look right, but it isn't. You can do better. Ruff the opening lead, draw trumps, and play the ♣A and ♣K. If the ♣Q falls (close to 20%) your ♣J is high, your thirteenth trick, the ♠Q going bye-bye on the ◇A. If the ♣Q doesn't drop, discard the ♣J on the ◇A and ruff a club. If clubs are 3-3, dummy's fourth club is your thirteenth trick. If clubs are 4-2, there is still the spade finesse.

When the smoke clears, all those chances add up to about a 75% grand slam, odds good enough to justify shooting the moon.

The West hand: ♠ K J 9 2 ♡ 5 ◇ J 10 8 7 3 2 ♣ Q 8
The East hand: ♠ 10 8 6 4 ♡ 6 ◇ K Q 9 4 ♣ 10 9 7 5

> ***Tip:***
> *Don't be too eager to dump a loser on an ace from dummy when you are void in the suit led. If you have time to dump the loser later, saving the ace may afford you the opportunity to discard a different loser instead.*

Testing the clubs by playing the ♣AK to see if the ♣Q dropped before discarding a club was the difference between making and going down in your grand slam!

The same technique would apply in a contract of 7♡ if dummy had ♣AQxx facing ♣Jxx. Trump the opening lead, draw trumps, and lead a club to the ♣Q. If the ♣Q wins, cash the ♣A to see whether the ♣K drops doubleton. If it does, no need to discard the winning ♣J on the ◇A. Discard a different loser instead. If the ♣K doesn't drop, discard the ♣J on the ◇A, ruff a club, and hope for 3-3 clubs. This hand is somewhat similar to Problem 47.

SOLUTION 67

♠ A
♡ A 6 5
◇ K 8 6 5 4 2
♣ 8 7 6

♠ K Q 3 2
♡ K J 4 2
◇ 9 3
♣ A K 5

A quick 1NT-3NT sequence ends with the ♠J lead from West. Plan the play.

You start with seven sure tricks and have chances for extra tricks in diamonds and hearts. The heart finesse can wait. Trying to establish your long side suit comes first while the ♡A is still in dummy as a later entry to the diamonds.

Your first play from dummy should be a low diamond. You are going to lose two diamond tricks, minimum, no matter what, so ducking the first round can't hurt. If East takes the trick, he will probably return a spade, a return that you can handle. A club shift won't hurt either, but a heart shift would not be pleasant. Your best bet is to insert the ♡J, and if that gets covered duck to preserve the ♡A in dummy as a later entry to the hoped-for established diamonds.

If West wins the first diamond trick, no shift can hurt you. Assuming a black-suit shift, win and lead a second diamond intending to play the ◇K, your best chance to set up the suit. You need diamonds to be 3-2 and West to have the ◇A (34%) to bring home the suit for four tricks, chalking up two overtricks while you're at it. However, if East has the ◇A, you will have to fall back on Plan B, the heart finesse. Not only do you need to find the ♡Q with East, but hearts will have to be 3-3 to provide the four tricks you now need, a scary 18%. The bottom line is that I've stuck you with a bit less than an even money contract.

The West hand: ♠J 10 9 7 ♡Q 10 8 3 ◇A Q 7 ♣J 9
The East hand: ♠8 6 5 4 ♡9 7 ◇J 10 ♣Q 10 4 3 2

Kxxxx(x)

xx

Axxxx(x)

xx

At notrump, ducking the first round of a suit holding a small doubleton facing Kxxxx(x) or Axxxx(x) is the way to start long-suit establishment. However, in either case you must have at least one *unassailable* side-suit dummy entry even to think of doing this.

SOLUTION 68 (*ADVANCED*)

♠ 3
♡ K 7 4 2
◇ Q 10 7 6
♣ A K Q 2

♠ A J 8
♡ A Q 6
◇ K J 9 8
♣ 10 6 5

After you open 1NT, partner bids 2♣ and you wind up in 3NT. You notice that 6◇ would have been a nice contract, but difficult to reach. West leads the ♠4 against your 3NT contract, East playing the ♠K. Plan the play in 3NT and forget 6◇! The literature is filled with stories of declarers who started to play the hand in the contract they wanted to be in rather than the one they were in!

Since spades appear to be 5-4, and you don't know who has the ◇A, there is no point in holding up. The only right time to hold up is when spades are 6-3 and *East* has the ◇A. So you win the ♠A. Now what?

You have seven top tricks, and if clubs and hearts can be brought in for four tricks each, then leading a risky diamond hoping West has the ◇A won't be necessary. Play clubs before hearts. Cash the ♣A and ♣K in case the ♣J is singleton or doubleton. If the ♣J drops, cash the ♣10 to unblock the suit. If the ♣J doesn't appear, cash a third club anyway and then three rounds of hearts (assuming everyone follows to the first two rounds).

If both suits come in for four tricks, you have taken the first nine tricks and can lead a diamond, playing for overtricks. If neither (or one) suit has come in for four tricks, lead a diamond, praying West has the ◇A.

The West hand: ♠Q 10 7 4 2 ♡J 9 5 ◇5 4 2 ♣J 8
The East hand: ♠K 9 6 5 ♡10 8 3 ◇A 3 ♣9 7 4 3

The key features of this hand are: (1) not holding up in spades; (2) playing clubs before hearts in case the ♣J drops, preserving the ♡K as an entry to the club suit after the suit has been unblocked; (3) not leading a dangerous diamond unless you are sure you don't have enough tricks in clubs and hearts to make your contract.

Speaking of playing the contract you want to be in and not the one you are in brings to mind a story Don Krauss told me. In a National Team event, the partnership had been bidding hearts, but wound up in 7NT. Dummy had two little diamonds and declarer had the ◇AKx. The spade lead was won by declarer, who then played the ◇A, ◇K and a low diamond, telling Don to trump it! 'I'd love to,' Don said.

PROBLEM 69

♠ 8 5 2
♡ A Q 5 2
♢ Q 4
♣ A J 5 2

♠ K Q 10
♡ K 4
♢ A 5 3
♣ K 10 9 6 3

Partner opens 1♣, and not having any clever methods to describe your hand, you leap to 3NT, a bid which tends to end auctions as it does this one. West leads the ♡J. Plan the play.

PROBLEM 70

♠ Q 10 5 4
♡ A K 10 6
♢ Q
♣ Q 10 3 2

♠ K J 3 2
♡ Q J 9 8 3
♢ K
♣ K 9 6

Partner opens 1♣ and raises your 1♡ response to 2♡. You like your hand and bid 4♡. West leads the ♠A and East plays the ♠7. West continues with the ♠6, East playing the ♠8. Hearts are not 4-0.

PROBLEM 71 (*ADVANCED*)

♠ A 6 4
♡ A J 3
◇ J 8 5 3
♣ K 10 9

♠ K J 2
♡ K Q 10 9 4
◇ 6
♣ A Q J 4

After partner opens 1◇ and you respond 1♡, superior bidding (yours) lands you in 6♡. Undaunted, West leads the ◇K and ◇A, East encouraging. Plan the play.

PROBLEM 72

♠ A J 9 7
♡ A Q 7 6 2
◇ 9
♣ K 7 5

♠ K Q 10 8
♡ 3
◇ A 8 6 5 2
♣ 6 4 3

You land in 4♠ after partner opens 1♡ and raises your 1♠ response to 3♠. West leads the ♣Q, holding the trick. When West continues with the ♣J you play low from dummy again, but no luck, West does not have a doubleton ace. Now a third club goes to East's ♣A and a mean-looking trump is returned at Trick 4. Plan the play.

SOLUTION 69

♠ 8 5 2
♡ A Q 5 2
♢ Q 4
♣ A J 5 2

♠ K Q 10
♡ K 4
♢ A 5 3
♣ K 10 9 6 3

Partner opens 1♣, and not having any clever methods to describe your hand, you leap to 3NT, a bid which tends to end auctions as it does this one. West leads the ♡J. Plan the play.

It looks easy enough. There are tricks galore… yet there is a danger. See it? The danger is the diamond suit. You are vulnerable to a diamond attack from West. But how can West get in? One way is with the ♠A, but you can't do anything about that. However, you don't want to give West any other chance to get in if you can help it. And you can. If you play clubs from the top and West has ♣Qxx, you will have to concede a club to West. At this point you only have eight tricks and if West shifts to a diamond and East has the ♢K you could go down on this hand.

This never has to happen. Win the ♡K, cash the ♣K and lead a club to the ♣J. If it loses to East, so what? If he plays a diamond, you just duck, and have two secure stoppers (not to mention your ninth trick). So you now have four club tricks, three hearts and the ♢A, and if necessary you can set up one spade trick before West can get in to lead a diamond.

The West hand: ♠A 4 ♡J 10 9 8 ♢10 9 7 6 ♣Q 8 7
The East hand: ♠J 9 7 6 3 ♡7 6 3 ♢K J 8 2 ♣4

Your problem suit is not always the suit that is led. You might be vulnerable to a switch to another suit from a particular opponent, called the *danger hand.* Your job is to keep the danger hand off lead for as long as possible. Directing a finesse into the *non-danger hand* (finessing the club into East) is the way to go.

SOLUTION 70

♠ Q 10 5 4
♡ A K 10 6
◇ Q
♣ Q 10 3 2

♠ K J 3 2
♡ Q J 9 8 3
◇ K
♣ K 9 6

Partner opens 1♣ and raises your 1♡ response to 2♡. You like your hand and bid 4♡. West leads the ♠A and East plays the ♠7. West continues with the ♠6, East playing the ♠8. Hearts are not 4-0.

How good are you at finding jacks, like the ♣J? Not to worry, you won't have to because it doesn't matter who has it. After winning the spade continuation, draw trumps, strip spades, and exit with a diamond, your *equal*-length side suit. Whoever wins has to broach clubs or give you a ruff and sluff.

Once either opponent leads a club, your worries are over as you can't lose more than one club trick. Even without such strong intermediate club spots, you should play the same way. Good things happen when the opponents break suits first.

Once again, using an equally-divided suit as your throw-in suit eliminates a guess in a critical suit. Finally, if an opponent leads a diamond after winning the ace, conceding a ruff and sluff, ruff in the longer club hand (dummy) and discard a club from the shorter club hand (your hand). And yes, if West had cashed the ◇A before leading a second spade, you would have had to dig out the ♣J all by your lonesome to make the contract.

The West hand: ♠A 6 ♡5 4 2 ◇A 9 5 4 3 ♣7 5 4
The East hand: ♠9 8 7 ♡7 ◇J 10 8 7 6 2 ♣A J 8

SOLUTION 71 (*ADVANCED*)

♠ A 6 4
♡ A J 3
♢ J 8 5 3
♣ K 10 9

♠ K J 2
♡ K Q 10 9 4
♢ 6
♣ A Q J 4

After partner opens 1♢ and you respond 1♡, superior bidding (yours) lands you in 6♡. Undaunted, West leads the ♢K and ♢A, East encouraging. Plan the play.

You have eleven top tricks and need one more. The spade finesse is one way of getting that extra trick, but surely you have been brainwashed by now into delaying finesses in equal length suits until much later. Look for something else!

But what else? There is the possibility that if you ruff another diamond the ♢Q will fall. If the ♢Q doesn't drop, trump another diamond or three diamonds in all. You wind up with *six* trump tricks, the three diamond ruffs in your hand plus three more trump tricks, the ♡KQ in your hand facing the ♡AJ3 in dummy. Twelve tricks: six hearts, four clubs and two spades. No spade finesse needed.

Start with the ♡K and ♡A. If hearts divide 3-2, you are practically home free. Ruff a diamond, cross to the ♣10 and ruff dummy's last diamond with your last trump. Now over to the ♠A and discard your ♠J on dummy's ♡J (a jack for a jack). You are left with the ♠K and good clubs. How sweet it is.

If hearts divide 4-1, forget the dummy reversal. You will set up a trump trick for the opponent holding four trumps. If hearts are 4-1, ruff one diamond in case the queen drops and if it doesn't, take the spade finesse.

How to recognize dummy reversals? Most deal with 5-3 trump fits, a singleton in the long trump hand, and at least one, more commonly two or three, high trump honors in dummy, plus a slow loser that you will eventually discard on dummy's third trump! After trumping three times in the closed hand, dummy has one more trump than you do. Use that trump (the ♡J) to discard your spade loser. All you need is a strong combined trump suit, dummy entries, 3-2 trumps, and the ability to recognize the situation (the hardest part!). Piece of cake.

The West hand: ♠Q 10 8 ♡8 5 ♢A K 4 2 ♣8 6 3 2
The East hand: ♠9 7 5 3 ♡7 6 2 ♢Q 10 9 7 ♣7 5

Try your luck at reversing the dummy if West shifts to a trump at Trick 2 assuming East-West have the hands you see. You can do it!

SOLUTION 72

♠ A J 9 7
♡ A Q 7 6 2
♢ 9
♣ K 7 5

♠ K Q 10 8
♡ 3
♢ A 8 6 5 2
♣ 6 4 3

You land in 4♠ after partner opens 1♡ and raises your 1♠ response to 3♠. West leads the ♣Q, holding the trick. When West continues with the ♣J you play low from dummy again, but no luck, West does not have a doubleton ace. Now a third club goes to East's ♣A and a mean-looking trump is returned at Trick 4. Plan the play.

It would have been so easy if East had not shifted to a trump. You could have crossruffed for ten tricks: two red aces plus four ruffs in each hand. But the trump lead has cut your crossruff count down to nine tricks: the spade trick you have just taken plus six spades made separately, for seven trump tricks plus two red aces for nine. To recover the trick that the trump shift has cost you, take the heart finesse. Assuming it works, cash the ♡A, discarding a diamond, and merrily trump diamonds and hearts back and forth for ten tricks.

The West hand: ♠5 ♡K 9 5 4 ♢Q 10 7 3 ♣Q J 10 8
The East hand: ♠6 4 3 2 ♡J 10 8 ♢K J 4 ♣A 9 2

Tip:

Count your side-suit winners plus your trump-suit winners before embarking on a crossruff. For example, without the trump shift on this hand, the heart finesse would be needless. Also, before crossruffing, cash side-suit winners early (the ♡A after the ♡Q wins). You could lose them otherwise.

PROBLEM 73

♠ J
♡ A K Q 3 2
♢ 9 8 5 4
♣ A Q 4

♠ A K Q 7 6 2
♡ 6 4
♢ K 10 3
♣ K 5

You open 1♠, partner responds 2♡ and you elect to rebid 3NT. This turns out just fine as it lands you in the good contract of 6NT, partner's next bid. West leads the ♣J. Plan the play.

PROBLEM 74

♠ 9 4 3
♡ J 9 4
♢ A Q 9 4
♣ K J 7

♠ A Q 6
♡ K 5 3
♢ K J 6 3
♣ A 10 4

If there ever was a 3NT hand that the whole world would get to, this is it. Both hands balanced and 28 HCP between them should be enough. We'll see. West leads the ♠5 to the ♠J and your ♠Q. Plan the play (diamonds are 3-2, West having two).

PROBLEM 75

♠ 8 6
♡ 7 5
♢ A J 8 7 4 3
♣ 7 3 2

♠ A Q
♡ A Q J 10 9 8
♢ 2
♣ A K Q J

Do you like your hand? I hope so! You open 2♣, partner bids 2♢, you bid 2♡ and partner bids 3♢. You try 4♣ and this gets you 4♡. Blackwood tells you partner has an ace and you just can't settle for less than 6♡. How bad can it be? West leads the ♢K. Plan the play.

PROBLEM 76 (*ADVANCED*)

♠ A 8 3
♡ A 6 4
♢ 8 6 5
♣ 6 5 4 3

♠ K 5 4
♡ K 3 2
♢ A Q 4 3
♣ A K Q

The whole world ends up in 3NT on this hand, but not many would make it. Would you? The opening lead is the ♣J. East follows with the ♣7. Plan the play.

SOLUTION 73

♠ J
♡ A K Q 3 2
♢ 9 8 5 4
♣ A Q 4

♠ A K Q 7 6 2
♡ 6 4
♢ K 10 3
♣ K 5

You open 1♠, partner responds 2♡ and you elect to rebid 3NT. This turns out just fine as it lands you in the good contract of 6NT, partner's next bid. West leads the ♣J. Plan the play.

For a start, do not play too quickly to Trick 1. If you do, it's all over before you get started. If spades are no worse than 4-2, you have twelve top tricks. Even if they are 5-1, you are still alive if hearts are 3-3. However, the spade suit is blocked, the alarm clock signal to be careful as entry problems may exist. *You must have a side-suit entry to the hand (your hand) that has length in the blocked suit.*

Win the ♣Q, blocking that suit while you're at it. This is the key play because the ♣K can be used as an entry back to your hand after you cash the ♠J and there are heart entries to dummy to get to the ♣A. Time to run your top spades, discarding diamonds from dummy and leaving dummy with the ♡AKQ3. Assuming spades are no worse than 4-2, either dummy is high if hearts are 3-3, or the player with four hearts takes the thirteenth trick.

If spades are 5-1, discard three diamonds on the ♠AKQ, enter dummy with a heart and hope hearts divide 3-3. You've reached about a 90% slam.

The West hand: ♠9 4 ♡9 8 ♢A Q J ♣J 10 9 7 3 2
The East hand: ♠10 8 5 3 ♡J 10 7 5 ♢7 6 2 ♣8 6

SOLUTION 74

♠ 9 4 3
♡ J 9 4
◇ A Q 9 4
♣ K J 7

♠ A Q 6
♡ K 5 3
◇ K J 6 3
♣ A 10 4

If there ever was a 3NT hand that the whole world would get to, this is it. Both hands balanced and 28 HCP between them should be enough. We'll see. West leads the ♠5 to the ♠J and your ♠Q. Plan the play (diamonds are 3-2, West having two).

You would hate to go down with 28 points between the two hands with stoppers galore. (I once went down with 31 HCP between the two hands — also with stoppers galore — and have yet to live it down! How could I, it was written up all over the place!)

Start by counting sure tricks. There are eight: four diamonds, two clubs and two spades. Of course there are chances for a ninth. You might try leading up to the ♡K and if that loses and a spade comes back you still have the club finesse in reserve. Or even leading a heart to the ♡9, playing West for the ♡10 and East for the ♡Q. All possible ways of getting a ninth trick. Sorry, no cigar.

There is a much better line, one that is overlooked time and again. Why? Because it goes against the grain to let an opponent in who has winners to cash. It's forgotten that after the fun and games are over, the eventual return will give you a trick, oftentimes the contract-fulfilling trick, as is the case here.

Play three rounds of diamonds leaving a higher diamond in dummy, and now the ♠A and another spade. Assuming East follows to the second spade, the most West can cash is three spades and you can handle that. You can discard two hearts from dummy and a heart and a club from your hand. West has only hearts and clubs left.

If West returns a heart, your ♡K is your ninth trick no matter who has the ace. If West returns a club, given your diamond entry in dummy, you have three club tricks after you play low from dummy. Start thinking 'throw-in' these days.

The West hand: ♠K 10 8 5 2 ♡A Q 6 ◇10 5 ♣8 3 2
The East hand: ♠J 7 ♡10 8 7 2 ◇8 7 2 ♣Q 9 6 5

SOLUTION 75

♠ 8 6
♡ 7 5
◇ A J 8 7 4 3
♣ 7 3 2

♠ A Q
♡ A Q J 10 9 8
◇ 2
♣ A K Q J

Do you like your hand? I hope so! You open 2♣, partner bids 2◇, you bid 2♡ and partner bids 3◇. You try 4♣ and this gets you 4♡. Blackwood tells you partner has an ace and you just can't settle for less than 6♡. How bad can it be? West leads the ◇K. Plan the play.

Mirror, mirror on the wall, which is the best finesse of all?

The better part of this book has practically begged you to postpone finesses in evenly-divided short side suits until later, much later. Well, this is bridge and there never was a rule that didn't have an exception. Ever.

You are in dummy for the *last* time and have to take the heart or the spade finesse. The spade finesse is clearly better. If it works, you give up a heart and that's the end of it — *one* finesse, 50%. If you lead a heart you will need to find East with a singleton or doubleton king (16%) as you can't repeat the finesse. Well, 50% is better than 16%. Rules are great, but the 'real' rule is to consider each hand as a separate entity and play accordingly.

The West hand: ♠J 9 4 3 2 ♡6 2 ◇K Q 10 9 ♣10 8
The East hand: ♠K 10 7 5 ♡K 4 3 ◇6 5 ♣9 6 5 4

SOLUTION 76 (ADVANCED)

♠ A 8 3
♡ A 6 4
♢ 8 6 5
♣ 6 5 4 3

♠ K 5 4
♡ K 3 2
♢ A Q 4 3
♣ A K Q

The whole world ends up in 3NT on this hand, but not many would make it. The opening lead is the ♣J. East follows with the ♣7. Plan the play.

You have eight top tricks with a chance for a ninth in clubs if they break 3-3, something you can discover later. Your main concern is securing two diamond tricks. It looks easy enough. If East has the ♢K, you can take at least two diamond tricks via a finesse. If diamonds are 3-3, you can always establish a second diamond trick no matter who has the king by playing the suit three times. But there is a 'best' way to go for two diamond tricks with this combination.

Play a low diamond from both hands at Trick 2! Say they win and shift to a heart. Win the king, cash the ♢A, and (assuming the ♢K hasn't dropped) cash a second club. If both follow, try a third club. Assuming clubs are not 3-3, cross to the ♠A and lead a diamond towards your Qx.

Why is this so great? This play wins whenever diamonds are 3-3, whenever *East* has the ♢K (any length), and also wins when *West* has a singleton or doubleton king (the reason why this play is better than an immediate finesse) — and let's not overlook an unlikely 3-3 club split.

The West hand: ♠J 9 7 ♡Q 8 5 ♢K 2 ♣J 10 9 8 2
The East hand: ♠Q 10 6 2 ♡J 10 9 7 ♢J 10 9 7 ♣7

You can apply somewhat the same technique with the following combination if you need *three* tricks and have a side-suit entry to dummy.

AJxx

? ?

Kxx

Play the ace and king and then lead low to the jack. You score three tricks whenever West has the queen, whenever East has Qx (an extra 16% — the pickup) or whenever the suit breaks 3-3.

PROBLEM 77

♠ K
♡ Q J 10 5
◇ 7 6 4 3
♣ Q J 10 5

♠ A Q J 10 9 7
♡ A 3
◇ A 5 2
♣ A 4

Aces galore. You open 1♠ and leap to 4♠ after partner responds 1NT. West leads the ◇Q, East signals encouragement with the ◇9. Plan the play.

PROBLEM 78

♠ J 10 3 2
♡ A 6
◇ 7 5 4
♣ A Q J 7

♠ A K Q 8 7
♡ Q 3
◇ Q 8 3
♣ K 9 4

Partner opens 1♣, East passes, you respond 1♠, West joins in with 3♡, vulnerable. Partner coughs up 3♠, you downgrade your ♡Q and conclude the auction with a 4♠ bid. West leads the ♡J (standard leads). Plan the play.

PROBLEM 79

♠ 7 6
♡ A 9 8 5 4
◇ K 6
♣ K J 9 2

♠ 10 2
♡ Q J 10 7 6
◇ A 8 3
♣ A 10 3

You like your hand enough to open 1♡. West overcalls 3♠ and partner's 4♡ bid ends the auction. West leads the ♠K, East overtakes and returns a spade to West's ♠J. At Trick 3 West exits with the ◇J. Plan the play.

PROBLEM 80

♠ 4 2
♡ J 10
◇ K 9 6 5
♣ A K 10 8 2

♠ 10 7
♡ A Q 6
◇ A Q J 10 3
♣ J 9 5

You open 1◇ and rebid 2◇ after partner's 2♣ response. After partner raises to 3◇, you try 3♡ looking for a spade stopper, and partner leaps to 5◇, the final contract. West leads the ♠K and then a spade to East's ♠A. East returns the inevitable heart and there you are. Plan the play.

SOLUTION 77

♠ K
♡ Q J 10 5
◇ 7 6 4 3
♣ Q J 10 5

♠ A Q J 10 9 7
♡ A 3
◇ A 5 2
♣ A 4

Aces galore. You open 1♠ and leap to 4♠ after partner responds 1NT. West leads the ◇Q, East signals encouragement with the ◇9. Plan the play.

A declarer who does not count sure tricks before embarking on the play is a scary partner. This hand is a good example. You have nine top tricks with finesse possibilities in two suits, clubs and hearts. However, to take a finesse in either suit, you must cross to the ♠K, using your only dummy entry. If the finesse loses, the opponents can cash their diamond tricks (it appears diamonds are 3-3 as East would have unblocked the ◇K with Kx) and exit safely with a spade or in your finesse suit as you are left with the blank ace. Don't look now, but you will be stuck in your hand with a loser in your other finesse suit, down one.

Since you need but one more trick to make your contract, make life easy for yourself. Win the ◇A and play the ♣A and another club or the ♡A and another heart. Yes, you are conceding a trick to the king, but at the same time you are setting up your tenth trick for a discard in your non-finesse suit while that friendly ♠K is still over there. For this line to work, you need the suit you are setting up to be divided 4-3 (62%), better than a 50% finesse. Count your tricks!

The West hand: ♠ 5 3 ♡ K 9 6 4 ◇ Q J 10 ♣ K 8 6 2
The East hand: ♠ 8 6 4 2 ♡ 8 7 2 ◇ K 9 8 ♣ 9 7 3

Notice that if you cross to dummy to take a club or a heart finesse, East's count signal will tell West that you only have one card left in the suit — the ace. By the way, you didn't think either of these finesses was actually going to work, did you?

Tip:
Before using the only entry to partner's hand to take a finesse, a finesse that will leave the suit blocked if it loses, consider attacking the suit without taking the finesse and using that 'only' entry to take a liberated trick in a suit you had the foresight not to block.

SOLUTION 78

♠ J 10 3 2
♡ A 6
◇ 7 5 4
♣ A Q J 7

♠ A K Q 8 7
♡ Q 3
◇ Q 8 3
♣ K 9 4

Partner opens 1♣, East passes, you respond 1♠, West joins in with 3♡, vulnerable. Partner coughs up 3♠, you downgrade your ♡Q and conclude the auction with a 4♠ bid. West leads the ♡J (standard leads). Plan the play.

There is not much to the play of this hand if you don't get greedy. Count your tricks! You have ten top tricks if you win the ♡A. Of course there is a strong chance that West has the ♡K, but you are not playing matchpoints here. These hands are designed to show you how to ensure contracts and *keep* partners, not how to risk contracts and lose them!

The West hand: ♠6 ♡J 10 9 8 7 5 4 ◇A J 10 ♣8 3
The East hand: ♠9 5 4 ♡K 2 ◇K 9 6 2 ♣10 6 5 2

Notice how greed strikes out on this layout. East would win the ♡K and shift to the ◇2 and the defense would collect the first four tricks. You would have to do quite a bit of explaining in the post-mortem.

Tip:

Playing matchpoints and given the 3♡ bid, vulnerable no less, it is worth the risk of losing your contract by playing low at Trick 1 to make an extra heart trick. However, if you know that West would not lead from a king at gunpoint, play the ace!

SOLUTION 79

♠ 7 6
♡ A 9 8 5 4
◇ K 6
♣ K J 9 2

♠ 10 2
♡ Q J 10 7 6
◇ A 8 3
♣ A 10 3

You like your hand enough to open 1♡. West overcalls 3♠ and partner's 4♡ bid ends the auction. West leads the ♠K, East overtakes and returns a spade to West's ♠J. At Trick 3 West exits with the ◇J. Plan the play.

You have finesse possibilities in two suits. First, let's talk about hearts. With ten hearts between your hand and dummy, the finesse is *far and away* the percentage play (76%). But when a throw-in play enters into the picture, the finesse is no longer the percentage play, the throw-in play is.

On this hand you can avoid both finesses! Win the ◇K and cash the ♡A. If both follow, claim! Lead a diamond to the ace, ruff a diamond, and exit a heart. Whoever has the king, probably East, will have to lead a club (or give you a ruff and sluff). Presto, no club loser.

If hearts are 3-0, you will have to find the ♣Q on your own. Since clubs is a two-way suit, think 'counting'. Your job is to count the other suits in order to determine which opponent started with more clubs originally and then play that opponent for the ♣Q.

The West hand: ♠K Q J 9 8 5 4 ♡2 ◇J 10 7 ♣Q 5
The East hand: ♠A 3 ♡K 3 ◇Q 9 5 4 2 ♣8 7 6 4

Life can be cruel when you misplay a hand. If you had to get a count on clubs (maybe you were distracted and took a heart finesse and it lost and a heart came back), you would discover that West started with two clubs and East four. Therefore, East is twice as likely to have the ♣Q so you should play East for the ♣Q. Not this time. It's sort of like being punished for being naughty.

SOLUTION 80

♠ 4 2
♡ J 10
♢ K 9 6 5
♣ A K 10 8 2

♠ 10 7
♡ A Q 6
♢ A Q J 10 3
♣ J 9 5

You open 1♢ and rebid 2♢ after partner's 2♣ response. After partner raises to 3♢, you try 3♡ looking for a spade stopper, and partner leaps to 5♢, the final contract. West leads the ♠K and then a spade to East's ♠A. East returns the inevitable heart and there you are. Plan the play.

We return to the wonderful, but diseased world of the 'practice finesse'. If you finesse the heart, even if it works, you still need the club finesse. But if the club finesse works, you don't need the heart finesse! Why take two finesses when one will do? Finessing the heart is a perfect example of a practice finesse. By the way, the definition of a practice finesse is this: if it works, it doesn't help, and if it loses it could cost the contract, not to mention one's partner. However, it does keep one in practice.

Win the ♡A, draw trumps, lead the ♣J to the ♣A, return to the closed hand with a trump and run the ♣9. Either you make the hand or you go down two. But at least you played it properly and, best of all, you didn't take a practice finesse!

The West hand: ♠K Q 9 3 ♡K 8 5 2 ♢8 7 ♣Q 7 6
The East hand: ♠A J 8 6 5 ♡9 7 4 3 ♢4 2 ♣4 3

PROBLEM 81 (*ADVANCED*)

♠ K 10 6 2
♡ K 2
♢ A 10 6 3
♣ A 5 4

♠ A J 4
♡ A Q 10 9 4 3
♢ 4 2
♣ 9 3

East opens 1♣, you overcall 1♡, West passes, and partner cuebids 2♣ looking for more information. You like your overcall so you jump to 3♡ and partner bids 4♡.

West leads the ♣2. You look at dummy and love your contract. You take the trick in dummy and play the ♡K and a heart to the ♡A, East discarding a club on the second heart. Suddenly love has turned to concern. How do you continue?

PROBLEM 82

♠ —
♡ Q 10 9 8 6 5
♢ Q J 9 7
♣ 8 6 2

♠ Q J 6 5
♡ A K J 7 3 2
♢ —
♣ A Q 5

With both sides vulnerable, you open 1♡ and here comes the chorus. West overcalls 2♡ showing spades and a minor, partner raises to 4♡, East chimes in with 4♠, and counting on partner to be short in spades, you put an end to this nonsense by bidding 6♡. West leads the ♠3. Plan the play.

PROBLEM 83

♠ 6 3
♡ A K Q 10 8
◇ K J 3 2
♣ 4 2

♠ A Q 2
♡ J 9
◇ A Q 10 9
♣ A Q 5 3

With only East-West vulnerable, West opens 2♠, weak, and partner overcalls 3♡. Facing a hand that figures to have a reasonable six-card suit for a vulnerable three-level overcall, plus opening bid values, you decide your 19 HCP, including a heart honor, is enough to risk a leap to 6NT. The opening lead is the ◇8, East following. Partner owes you a heart, but the 3♡ bid is certainly reasonable. In any case you start with eleven top tricks with chances for a twelfth in the blacks. Plan the play.

PROBLEM 84

♠ A Q J 10
♡ A Q 9
◇ 4 3
♣ 10 4 3 2

♠ 4 2
♡ K J 10 8 7 4 2
◇ Q 9 8
♣ K

East opens 1♣, you overcall 3♡, West passes, and partner raises to 4♡ ending the bidding. West leads the ♣Q to East's ♣A and East continues with the ◇K, ◇A and ◇10 to your ◇Q. Plan the play.

♠ K 10 6 2
♡ K 2
◇ A 10 6 3
♣ A 5 4

♠ A J 4
♡ A Q 10 9 4 3
◇ 4 2
♣ 9 3

East opens 1♣, you overcall 1♡, West passes, and partner cuebids 2♣ looking for more information. You like your overcall so you jump to 3♡ and partner bids 4♡. West leads the ♣2. You look at dummy and love your contract. You take the trick in dummy and play the ♡K and a heart to the ♡A, East discarding a club on the second heart. How do you continue?

You are faced with a possible loser in each suit. Thankfully dummy has good spades, so if you do this right, you can get rid of a diamond on a spade — even if you have a spade loser. 'Doing this right' means cashing the ♡Q, leaving the ♡J at large, and now the key plays — the ♠A, ♠K and ♠J. No finesse! Why? If you look at the East-West hands it may be easier to see why.

The West hand: ♠8 3 ♡J 8 6 5 ◇J 8 7 5 ♣10 6 2
The East hand: ♠Q 9 7 5 ♡7 ◇K Q 9 ♣K Q J 8 7

Though it is likely that East has the ♠Q, it is *not* clear. Let's go back to the suggested line. East wins the ♠Q, cashes a club, and shifts to the ◇K, which you win with dummy's ◇A. Now you can discard your losing diamond on dummy's ♠10. If West ruffs, it is with a natural trump trick so nothing is lost. You make your contract losing one heart, one spade and one club.

Now let's see what happens if you take a spade finesse into East and it loses. A club is cashed and now comes the diamond shift to dummy's ◇A. Now when you try to get rid of your diamond loser on dummy's spades, West trumps the *third* spade and a diamond is cashed for down one. The same fate would befall you if took a spade finesse into West and it lost. Again you would be at the mercy of 3-3 spades.

This may not be easy to 'see', but if the player with four hearts has two spades, you can't afford to take a losing finesse in *either* direction. If you do, you will not have time to get rid of your diamond loser on a fourth spade. However, if you lose a *third*-round spade trick, no matter who has the ♠Q you will be able to discard your diamond loser on a fourth spade, losing three tricks in all.

SOLUTION 82

♠ —
♡ Q 10 9 8 6 5
♢ Q J 9 7
♣ 8 6 2

♠ Q J 6 5
♡ A K J 7 3 2
♢ —
♣ A Q 5

With both sides vulnerable, you open 1♡ and here comes the chorus. West overcalls 2♡ showing spades and a minor, partner raises to 4♡, East chimes in with 4♠, and counting on partner to be short in spades, you put an end to this nonsense by bidding 6♡. West leads the ♠3. Plan the play.

Well, you were right about partner being short in spades, but you still have two possible club losers to deal with. Of course you can always take the club finesse, but not so fast. East clearly has the ♠A and West figures to have the ♠K. Keep in mind that West does not have the ♢AK (he didn't lead the suit) making it even more likely he has the ♠K for his vulnerable 2♡ bid.

Do yourself a favor: discard a club from dummy at Trick 1 and let East win the ace. East will surely switch to a club and now is the moment of truth. Win the ♣A, draw their lone trump and lead the ♠Q through West. Assuming West has the ♠K (he'll have it, he'll have it) you can discard dummy's remaining club on the ♠J.

The West hand: ♠K 10 8 3 2 ♡— ♢A 10 5 4 3 ♣K 9 3
The East hand: ♠A 9 7 4 ♡4 ♢K 8 6 2 ♣J 10 7 4

Repeat reminder: As declarer, when you have a strong holding in the suit led lacking the ace, and dummy has a void, you usually gain a trick (or two) by discarding a slow loser from dummy rather than trumping. The gain comes when you get to discard yet another loser or two on the honors in your hand that have been promoted after the ace wins on your right.

Tip:

As declarer, missing the ace-king of a side suit that is not led, assume the opening leader does not have both honors. In a suit contract, if a low card is led, assume the ace is to your right and the king to your left, particularly if the opening leader has bid the suit. However, if third hand wins the trick with the king, assume he has the ace as well. Aces are seldom underled in suit contracts.

SOLUTION 83

♠ 6 3
♡ A K Q 10 8
♢ K J 3 2
♣ 4 2

♠ A Q 2
♡ J 9
♢ A Q 10 9
♣ A Q 5 3

With only East-West vulnerable, West opens 2♠, weak, and partner overcalls 3♡. Facing a hand that figures to have a reasonable six-card suit for a vulnerable three-level overcall, plus opening bid values, you decide your 19 HCP, including a heart honor, is enough to risk a leap to 6NT. The opening lead is the ♢8, East following. Partner owes you a heart, but the 3♡ bid is certainly reasonable. In any case you start with eleven top tricks with chances for a twelfth in the blacks. Plan the play.

It is very likely that West has both black kings to justify a first seat vulnerable vs. not 2♠ opening bid. After all, between your hand and dummy, you have everything else.

The idea is to cash all nine of your red-suit winners ending in dummy. This leaves dummy with two small black doubletons and you have the AQ doubleton in each black suit.

Your play at this point depends upon how many spades West has discarded, keeping in mind he figures to have started with six. If West has discarded four spades, he will be down to the ♠KJ doubleton and two clubs. Play the ♠A and ♠Q and take the last two tricks no matter who has the ♣K.

If West has discarded only three spades, then West is down to three spades, probably headed by the ♠KJ, and a singleton club, probably the ♣K. No matter. Lead a club to the ♣Q. Even if West wins a singleton ♣K, he must lead a spade now and you take the last three tricks.

Once you are pretty sure who holds the missing important honors, a throw-in play rather than a finesse is often a more attractive option.

The West hand: ♠ K J 10 8 7 4 ♡ 6 4 ♢ 8 7 ♣ K J 7
The East hand: ♠ 9 5 ♡ 7 5 3 2 ♢ 6 5 4 ♣ 10 9 8 6

SOLUTION 84

♠ A Q J 10
♡ A Q 9
♢ 4 3
♣ 10 4 3 2

♠ 4 2
♡ K J 10 8 7 4 2
♢ Q 9 8
♣ K

East opens 1♣, you overcall 3♡, West passes, and partner raises to 4♡ ending the bidding. West leads the ♣Q to East's ♣A and East continues with the ♢K, ♢A and ♢10 to your ♢Q. Plan the play.

The idea is not to put all of your eggs in the spade finesse basket too quickly. You have another chance. If West started with the ♣QJ(x) and you trump a club or two, the ♣10 may set up for a spade discard. It can't hurt to try.

It actually doesn't matter if you trump the ♢Q or discard a spade from dummy. What you can't do is discard a club! Say you discard a spade, cross to dummy with the ♡A and trump a club, and nothing exciting happens. Don't give up. Return to dummy with the ♡Q and trump a second club. If the ♣J appears, no spade finesse will be necessary. If it doesn't appear, take the spade finesse.

Trumping a few cards in a relatively weak side suit (here, clubs) headed by a secondary honor (here, the ♣10) can produce spectacular results, particularly when several honors in the suit have already been played. In this case three club honors bit the dust at Trick 1.

Believe it or not, if dummy had the ♣9432, there would still be a tiny chance that the ♣9 would become high. 'All' you need is to find West with the ♣QJ10 alone. Never give up!

The West hand: ♠9 6 5 3 ♡5 ♢J 7 6 5 2 ♣Q J 9
The East hand: ♠K 8 7 ♡6 3 ♢A K 10 ♣A 8 7 6 5

PROBLEM 85 (*ADVANCED*)

♠ Q
♡ K 10
♢ A 9 7 4 3
♣ A K 10 3 2

♠ A K 8 7 5 4 3
♡ A 6 2
♢ 5
♣ J 9

Sit tight! Partner opens 1♢, you respond 1♠, partner bids 2♣ and you leap to 4♠ showing an opening bid with strong spades. Partner tries 4NT, you show three keycards and partner bids 7♠ hoping (praying) that the ♠Q solidifies your spades. (There should be a way to ask for the trump jack.) Wild stabs like this can be hard on the central nervous system, in this case yours! So your contract is 7♠ and the lead is the ♡Q. Plan the play.

PROBLEM 86

♠ 7
♡ J 3
♢ A Q 10
♣ A K Q 7 6 3 2

♠ Q 10 6
♡ A K 5 4 2
♢ J 8 4 3 2
♣ —

Partner opens 1♣ and jumps to 3♣ over your 1♡ response. You decide to conceal your diamonds and bid 3NT, ending the auction. West leads the ♠3, East plays the ♠A and returns the ♠4. You insert the ♠10, driving out West's ♠K (one bullet dodged). West gets out with the ♠2 to East's ♠J and your ♠Q. What two discards have you made from dummy and where do you go from here?

PROBLEM 87

♠ K 9
♡ A J 10 9 7 5
◇ J 6 3
♣ 7 5

♠ A J 4 2
♡ K Q
◇ 5 4 2
♣ A Q J 6

After you open 1NT, partner responds 4◇, a transfer to hearts, and passes your forced 4♡ bid. West starts with the ◇A, ◇K and ◇Q, East showing four, and exits a trump, East following. Plan the play.

PROBLEM 88

♠ 7 6
♡ K J 3
◇ A 6 5 2
♣ K 7 5 4

♠ 10 8 3
♡ A 10 9 8 4 2
◇ 10 8
♣ A 9

Fate has propelled you into a 19 HCP game contract. Here's what happened:

West opened 2♠, weak, passed around to you, and you balanced with 3♡. Partner can hardly be blamed for bidding 4♡, so there you are. The opening lead is the ♠K. East overtakes and returns a spade to West who plays a third high spade. Plan the play.

SOLUTION 85 (*ADVANCED*)

♠ Q
♡ K 10
◇ A 9 7 4 3
♣ A K 10 3 2

♠ A K 8 7 5 4 3
♡ A 6 2
◇ 5
♣ J 9

Sit tight! Partner opens 1◇, you respond 1♠, partner bids 2♣ and you leap to 4♠ showing an opening bid with strong spades. Partner tries 4NT, you show three keycards and partner bids 7♠ hoping (praying) that the ♠Q solidifies your spades. So your contract is 7♠ and the lead is the ♡Q. Plan the play.

Your first thought should be that you can't make the hand if spades are 4-1, so assume a 3-2 division, a comforting thought. Now count your tricks! You have seven spades, two hearts, two clubs and a diamond for twelve. Since you can't afford to ruff a heart in dummy with the ♠Q, you are going to have to set up your extra needed trick in either clubs or diamonds. Clubs look more promising, but looks can be deceiving.

It is dangerous to work with clubs before you draw trumps for fear of an uppercut or an overruff if clubs are a likely 4-2 (48%). And if you draw trumps first, you will only have one dummy entry left when you attack clubs. If clubs are 4-2 and the ♣Q doesn't drop, you are looking at a heart loser.

There is a better way. Win the ♡A, saving the ♡K as a later dummy entry, cross to the ♠Q and now cash the ◇A and take a diamond ruff. That should be fairly safe. Next play the ♠AK discarding *two clubs* from dummy. Not a misprint. Patience.

Cross to the ♣K, leading the ♣J to unblock the suit in case you want to finesse the ten later, and ruff a second diamond. If both follow, meaning diamonds were 4-3 (62%), the opponents have only one diamond left. You have two dummy entries, the ♡K and the ♣A, so you can easily establish dummy's fifth diamond for your thirteenth trick.

If diamonds break 5-2, you still have the club finesse to fall back on. But before leading a club, keep this in mind: When you have all the tricks but one, cash *all* of your trumps before leading the ♣9. Strange and wonderful things may develop, like a squeeze or an errant discard(s). *Just do it!*

The West hand: ♠J 6 2 ♡Q J 9 4 3 ◇K J 6 ♣8 4
The East hand: ♠10 9 ♡8 7 5 ◇Q 10 8 2 ♣Q 7 6 5

SOLUTION 86

♠ 7
♡ J 3
◇ A Q 10
♣ A K Q 7 6 3 2

♠ Q 10 6
♡ A K 5 4 2
◇ J 8 4 3 2
♣ —

Partner opens 1♣ and jumps to 3♣ over your 1♡ response. You decide to conceal your diamonds and bid 3NT, ending the auction. West leads the ♠3, East plays the ♠A and returns the ♠4. You insert the ♠10, driving out West's ♠K (one bullet dodged). West gets out with the ♠2 to East's ♠J and your ♠Q. What two discards have you made from dummy and where do you go from here?

You dare not give up the lead, and must decide whether to rely on clubs to come in for seven tricks or take the diamond finesse. If the diamond finesse works, you have at least nine tricks. You can't do both because you don't have a club in your hand to test the suit and then fall back on the diamond finesse if clubs don't break 3-3.

What are the numbers? Crossing to the ◇A and playing clubs requires 3-3 clubs (36%) or finding the ◇K singleton (5%) for a grand total of about 41%. The diamond finesse is 50%, so that should decide the issue. Discard a club and a heart from dummy and lead a low diamond to the ◇Q. If it holds, cash the ♣A, ♣K and ♣Q, discarding hearts (maybe they'll break 3-3!). If they don't, cash the ♡A and ♡K and lead a second low diamond. If the king appears, you have the rest, if it doesn't, insert the ◇10 and settle for nine tricks.

Knowing that a simple finesse is a better chance for success than a 3-3 break is the key to the play of this hand.

The West hand: ♠K 9 8 3 2 ♡10 7 ◇K 9 6 5 ♣10 8
The East hand: ♠A J 5 4 ♡Q 9 8 6 ◇7 ♣J 9 5 4

Don't be seduced by a beautiful side suit such as AKQxxxx facing a void or AKQxxx facing a singleton. Chances are the suit is not going to run, so look around for a Plan B in case it doesn't.

SOLUTION 87

♠ K 9
♡ A J 10 9 7 5
◇ J 6 3
♣ 7 5

♠ A J 4 2
♡ K Q
◇ 5 4 2
♣ A Q J 6

After you open 1NT, partner responds 4◇, a transfer to hearts, and passes your forced 4♡ bid. West starts with the ◇A, ◇K and ◇Q, East showing four, and exits a trump, East following. Plan the play.

We've seen this theme before. When there is a choice of two finesses, one missing a queen and one missing a king, you normally play the ace-king of the suit missing the queen hoping the queen drops, and if it doesn't, take the finesse in the suit missing the king. However, when the suit missing the queen includes a doubleton on one side, you can increase your chances by not only playing the ace-king, but also by trumping a small card in the suit hoping someone has Qxx (37%). On a good day you won't need to take the club finesse at all.

Therefore the correct line is to draw trumps, discarding two *clubs* from your hand if hearts break 4-1, and then play the ♠K and ♠A and trump a spade. If the queen has appeared, you won't need the club finesse as the ♠J takes care of the club loser. If the ♠Q doesn't show up, take the club finesse, a near 70% contract if you play spades before clubs.

The West hand: ♠ Q 6 3 ♡ 8 4 3 2 ◇ A K Q 7 ♣ K 10
The East hand: ♠ 10 8 7 5 ♡ 6 ◇ 10 9 8 ♣ 9 8 4 3 2

SOLUTION 88

♠ 7 6
♡ K J 3
◇ A 6 5 2
♣ K 7 5 4

♠ 10 8 3
♡ A 10 9 8 4 2
◇ 10 8
♣ A 9

West opened 2♠, weak, passed around to you and you balanced with 3♡. Partner can hardly be blamed for bidding 4♡, so there you are. The opening lead is the ♠K. East overtakes and returns a spade to West who plays a third high spade. Plan the play.

You can trump with the ♡J, winning whenever West has the ♡Q but losing when East has the ♡Q. Or you can trump with the ♡K and run the ♡J winning whenever East has the ♡Q but losing whenever West has the ♡Q. Is one appreciably better than the other? Is the Pope Catholic? West started with six spades and has seven 'other' cards; East has eleven 'other' cards. Chances are that East with *eleven* other cards has the ♡Q. Ruff with the ♡K and run the ♡J through East.

You can even make this hand if East started with all four hearts! After ruffing with the ♡K and running the ♡J, lead a low heart to the ♡8. Now the idea is to shorten your trump holding twice, reducing to the same heart length as East, two. Play the ♣A and ♣K and trump a club, then cross to the ◇A and trump another club. You now have the ♡A10 and the ◇10. Exit with the diamond and take the last two tricks with the ♡A10. You reduce so beautifully.

The West hand: ♠K Q J 5 4 2 ♡5 ◇Q 9 3 ♣J 6 2
The East hand: ♠A 9 ♡Q 7 6 ◇K J 7 4 ♣Q 10 8 3

Tip

Length attracts shortness and shortness attracts length.

Tip

When your RHO has a trump honor that can be finessed and dummy is void in trumps, all is not lost. If you can manage to reduce to the same trump length as your opponent, cash your side-suit winners and then give up whatever loser(s) you may have. If you have no side-suit loser, arrange to end up in dummy at Trick 11. Either way, you will take the last two trump tricks.

PROBLEM 89

♠ A 10 8 7
♡ K Q 10
◇ 9 8 7 4
♣ K 6

♠ K Q J 9 4 2
♡ —
◇ A 10 3 2
♣ A J 3

Partner has convinced you to play a Weak 1NT opening bid showing 12-14 HCP and then pulls one out of the hat fifteen minutes later. Since you don't know all the responses, rather than have a soul-searching auction you bid what you hope you can make, six spades. West leads the ♡3. Plan the play. Spades are 2-1.

PROBLEM 90

♠ 10 9 8 6
♡ K 6 2
◇ Q J
♣ A 7 4 2

♠ A Q J 5 4
♡ A 5 4
◇ K 7 4
♣ Q J

You have no trouble getting to 4♠ after partner makes a limit raise of your 1♠ opening bid. West leads the ♡3, fourth best. Plan the play.

PROBLEM 91 (*ADVANCED*)

♠ A 8 6 5
♡ A K 6
◇ 4
♣ K 7 6 4 3

♠ K 7 4 3
♡ 7 5 3
◇ J 6 2
♣ A J 5

Partner opens 1♣ and jump raises your 1♠ response to 3♠. You bid 4♠. West leads the ◇K and shifts to the ♡10. You win in dummy and play the ♠K and ♠A. Spades are 3-2. Plan the play.

PROBLEM 92

♠ K 9 3
♡ J 9 4 2
◇ J 10 6
♣ A Q 7

♠ A J 2
♡ K Q 10 7 6
◇ 8 5
♣ K 9 5

West opens 1♠, passed around to you. You try 2♡, partner raises to 3♡ and you battle on with 4♡. West leads the ◇K, East encourages and West continues with the ◇Q and another diamond to East's ◇A as you trump. When you play a low heart, West takes the ♡A and exits a heart, East following. Plan the play.

SOLUTION 89

♠ A 10 8 7
♡ K Q 10
◇ 9 8 7 4
♣ K 6

♠ K Q J 9 4 2
♡ —
◇ A 10 3 2
♣ A J 3

Partner has convinced you to play a Weak 1NT opening bid showing 12-14 HCP. Since you don't know all the responses, rather than have a soul-searching auction you bid what you hope you can make, six spades. West leads the ♡3. Plan the play. Spades are 2-1.

Your only losers are in diamonds. You can discard one diamond from your hand on a heart if you play the ♡Q from dummy, but that still leaves you with two diamond losers. A far better play is the ♡10 at Trick 1. If West has led from the ♡J, the ♡10 drives out the ♡A and you can discard *two* diamonds on the ♡KQ.

Say you 'accidentally' played the ♡Q at Trick 1, East played the ♡A and you ruffed. It doesn't look good as you are staring at two diamond losers. However, when you have losers in just one suit and have the wherewithal to strip the hand before you play that suit, do it! *Do it!*

Draw two rounds of trumps ending in dummy, discard a diamond on the ♡K, ruff the ♡10, stripping that suit, and then play the ♣K and ♣A and ruff the ♣J in dummy, stripping that suit as well (the club finesse does you no good as you can only discard one meaningless diamond from dummy if it works). The stage is set. Lead a diamond to your ◇A and exit a diamond. What good will this do? Well, diamonds might be blocked. One defender may have the ◇KQ, ◇KJ, or ◇QJ doubleton and will have to concede a ruff and sluff upon winning the trick.

The West hand: ♠5 ♡J 9 7 3 2 ◇K J 6 ♣10 7 5 4
The East hand: ♠6 3 ♡A 8 6 5 4 ◇Q 5 ♣Q 9 8 2

And there is another possible winning scenario. Look at the East-West hands. West has the ◇KJ6 and East the ◇Q5. When you lead a second diamond from your hand, West must play the ◇K, not the ◇J! If West plays the ◇J, East wins the ◇Q and you get a ruff and sluff! Yes, West should play the ◇K when you exit a diamond as you wouldn't be playing this way with the ◇Q, but West may be sleepy or not be that sharp. Playing the king is called the Crocodile Coup — like a crocodile opening its jaws to swallow partner's blocking honor!

SOLUTION 90

♠ 10 9 8 6
♡ K 6 2
♢ Q J
♣ A 7 4 2

♠ A Q J 5 4
♡ A 5 4
♢ K 7 4
♣ Q J

You have no trouble getting to 4♠ after partner makes a limit raise of your 1♠ opening bid. West leads the ♡3, fourth best. Plan the play.

Optimistically, you could make an overtrick if both black finesses work. Realistically, you could go down if both finesses lose — and you misplay the hand.

Your first concern should be that 'slow' heart loser. If the opponents get in twice before you can get rid of your heart loser, that slow heart loser becomes a fast heart loser. Worse, you could go down if both black kings are offside. The bottom line is that you don't have 'time' to take the spade finesse. If it loses and a heart comes back, down you go if the club finesse also loses.

What you have to do is start with one of the minor suits to get rid of your slow heart loser, but which one? And did you notice that both minor suits are blocked? When you see a blocked suit, think *entries*. After a suit has been unblocked, there must be an entry to the hand where the established trick(s) resides.

Say you win the ♡A in hand and try the club finesse — it loses and a heart comes back driving out dummy's ♡K. After you unblock the ♣J you can't get back to dummy to cash the ♣A unless the ♠K is singleton. Don't hold your breath.

Now look at the other blocked suit, diamonds. Say you win the opening lead in *dummy* with the ♡K, drive out the ♢A, and another heart comes back driving out your ♡A. Good defense, but you will prevail. Unblock the ♢J and cross to the ♠A — no finesse please! Why put your contract at risk for no good reason? After the ♠A, cash the ♢K, discarding a heart from dummy. Assuming nothing too cruel has happened like someone trumping the ♢K with a small spade and East having the ♣K to boot, you are home free, losing a diamond, a spade, maybe a club, but not a heart.

The West hand: ♠K 3 ♡Q 10 8 3 ♢A 8 6 2 ♣10 8 3
The East hand: ♠7 2 ♡J 9 7 ♢10 9 5 3 ♣K 9 6 5

Getting rid of a slow loser usually boils down to winning a race. Can they set up a trick in your slow loser suit before you can get rid of it safely?

SOLUTION 91 (*ADVANCED*)

♠ A 8 6 5
♡ A K 6
♢ 4
♣ K 7 6 4 3

♠ K 7 4 3
♡ 7 5 3
♢ J 6 2
♣ A J 5

Partner opens 1♣ and jump raises your 1♠ response to 3♠. You bid 4♠. West leads the ♢K and shifts to the ♡10. You win in dummy and play the ♠K and ♠A. Spades are 3-2. Plan the play.

You have arrived at a neat 22 HCP game and fortunately spades are 3-2. Can you play the hand relatively safely? After all, you are in some danger of losing a trick in each suit.

The idea is to set up the club suit for a heart discard *before* the opponents can cash a heart trick, a slow loser. Once again you are involved in a race! If you make the more or less normal play of taking the club finesse and it loses, a heart will come back. Now you must cash the ♣A and ♣K and hope the third club lives. If it does not, the player who trumps can cash a heart trick, the setting trick. Scary.

The idea is not to give the player with the third trump a chance to trump a *third* round of clubs in case the club finesse loses. In order to avoid that disappointment, give up on the club finesse and play the ♣A, ♣K and another club as if you didn't have the ♣J! The ♣J is an illusion when spades are 3-2. Assuming 3-2 clubs and no ♣Q doubleton, someone will win the ♣Q and play a second heart. Now you are in charge. Discard your losing heart on the fourth round of clubs. You have just won the race. A similar race took place on Problem 81. How many of these races did you win?

If spades are 4-1, you need East to have the ♣Q and clubs to be 3-2.

The West hand: ♠J 2 ♡10 9 2 ♢K Q 9 8 7 ♣Q 10 2
The East hand: ♠Q 10 9 ♡Q J 8 4 ♢A 10 5 3 ♣9 8

SOLUTION 92

♠ K 9 3
♡ J 9 4 2
◇ J 10 6
♣ A Q 7

♠ A J 2
♡ K Q 10 7 6
◇ 8 5
♣ K 9 5

West opens 1♠, passed around to you. You try 2♡, partner raises to 3♡ and you battle on with 4♡. West leads the ◇K, East encourages and West continues with the ◇Q and another diamond to East's ◇A as you trump. When you play a low heart, West takes the ♡A and exits a heart, East following. Plan the play.

This is a one-suited problem. You have to avoid a spade loser and you know West has the ♠Q. East has already turned up with the ◇A and would not pass the 1♠ opening bid with 6 HCP.

If West has the ♠Q10, you have no chance. You have to assume East has the ♠10, probably doubleton. Cash the ♠A and run the ♠J through West hoping to drop that ♠10 on your right. What else can you do?

The West hand: ♠Q 8 7 6 4 ♡A 5 ◇K Q 9 ♣J 8 6
The East hand: ♠10 5 ♡8 3 ◇A 7 4 3 2 ♣10 4 3 2

Here is a somewhat analogous position:

Say you *know* that West has the ♠Q. Your best bet is to play East for the ♠10 and lead the ♠J. Say West covers. You win the ♠A and then lead low to the ♠9. You have just pulled off a 'backwards finesse'. The play of leading the ♠J from ♠KJx also works when dummy has the ♠A98. Ditto with ♠KJ8 facing ♠A9x, East having the ♠10 with *any* length. Clearly, the bidding may affect the play of even a common card combination. Stay flexible!

Tip:

If a player passes partner's opening bid and turns up with an ace, don't look for much else in that player's hand — a jack, maybe.

PROBLEM 93

♠ J 9
♡ K 7 6 4 3
◇ J 2
♣ A J 7 4

♠ A K Q 10 8 4
♡ A 5 2
◇ 8 4 3
♣ 9

You open 1♠ in fourth seat. Partner responds 2♡, you jump to 3♠ and partner bids 4♠. The opening lead is the ♣2. Plan the play.

PROBLEM 94

♠ A Q 7 5
♡ 6 2
◇ J 7 3
♣ A 10 5 4

♠ K 2
♡ A 10 8 5 3
◇ K 4
♣ K Q J 2

You talk yourself into opening 1NT because you want to protect your kings in case the contract ends up in notrump. Besides, you like playing the hand. Partner bids 2♣ and you bid 3♡, showing five hearts. Partner, not impressed, bids 3NT. West leads the ♠J. Plan the play.

PROBLEM 95

♠ 7
♡ K J 6 4
♢ Q 8 7 3 2
♣ A Q 5

♠ A 6 2
♡ 9
♢ A K J 9 6 5
♣ 6 4 3

You open 1♢, partner responds 1♡, East overcalls 1♠, you try 2♢, and West jumps to 3♠, preemptive. Partner has heard enough and leaps to 5♢, the final bid. West leads a disconcerting ♣J. Plan the play (diamonds are 1-1).

PROBLEM 96

♠ A K 5 4 2
♡ 7 3
♢ J 6 5
♣ Q J 7

♠ J 9
♡ A Q
♢ A K 10 9 8
♣ K 4 3 2

You open 1♢, partner responds 1♠, East throws in a vulnerable 2♡ overcall, you try 2NT showing 17-18 HCP and partner bids 3NT. West leads the ♡2 to East's ♡K and your ♡A. Yes, a rank beginner can make this hand if East has the ♢Q but what if he doesn't? What if West has the ♢Q and returns a second heart? What then? Plan the play.

SOLUTION 93

♠ J 9
♡ K 7 6 4 3
◇ J 2
♣ A J 7 4

♠ A K Q 10 8 4
♡ A 5 2
◇ 8 4 3
♣ 9

You open 1♠ in fourth seat. Partner responds 2♡, you jump to 3♠ and partner bids 4♠. The opening lead is the ♣2. Plan the play.

Counting top tricks you have nine: six spades, two hearts and the ♣A. You must contrive a way to get a tenth. There are two possibilities: (1) trying to trump a diamond in dummy; (2) working with the hearts in order to discard at least one diamond.

In order to trump a diamond in dummy, you must give up the lead twice. The opponents can see what you are doing and can thwart your plan by leading a trump each time they get in. The better plan is to work with hearts, a long suit that has a certain loser.

In order to keep control of the hand and the suit, duck a heart a Trick 2. If hearts are 3-2 (68%), you are home free. The best the opponents can do is take two diamond tricks, but that's all she wrote. You can win any return, draw trumps, and take the rest of the tricks.

When dealing with a side suit that is divided 5-3, the honors divided or both honors in the long hand (AKxxx), and you wish to keep control of the suit and the hand, duck the *first* round of the suit. On this hand if you incorrectly try to set up the hearts by playing the ♡A, ♡K and another, you won't be able to use your two established hearts because you can't draw trumps *ending* in dummy, the key to long-suit establishment when there is no side-suit entry to dummy.

The West hand: ♠7 6 5 ♡J 9 ◇A Q 6 5 ♣Q 8 6 2
The East hand: ♠3 2 ♡Q 10 8 ◇K 10 9 7 ♣K 10 5 3

Tip:

When planning to ruff a loser(s) in the short hand, assume the opponents will lead a trump each time they get in. This allows you to work out how many losers, if any, you can trump. If that plan won't gel, look around for something else, like a long side suit.

SOLUTION 94

♠ A Q 7 5
♡ 6 2
◇ J 7 3
♣ A 10 5 4

♠ K 2
♡ A 10 8 5 3
◇ K 4
♣ K Q J 2

You talk yourself into opening 1NT because you want to protect your kings in case the contract ends up in notrump. Besides, you like playing the hand. Partner bids 2♣ and you bid 3♡, showing five hearts. Partner, not impressed, bids 3NT. West leads the ♠J. Plan the play.

You start with eight sure tricks and must look to a red suit for a ninth. If you attack hearts, you more or less have to find hearts 3-3 (36%). If they are 4-2 (48%) the opponents may be able to establish a spade trick before you can set up your fifth heart not to mention the ◇A. In other words, if hearts are 4-2, your chances of success are remote with a capital 'R'.

What about diamonds, your weakest suit? It may be a weak suit, but it still offers you a 75% chance of getting one trick! Lead up to the ◇K and, if that loses, lead up to the ◇J — that's two finesses. You have to find the ◇A with East or the ◇Q with West. At times the shortest combined suit offers the best percentage chance of building up a quick trick. However, don't try to make a living playing short suits before long suits!

The West hand: ♠J 10 9 6 ♡Q 9 ◇A Q 5 2 ♣9 7 6
The East hand: ♠8 4 3 ♡K J 7 4 ◇10 9 8 6 ♣8 3

Tip:

Though it may work once in while, don't make a practice of opening 1NT with 5-4-2-2 distribution, particularly when the five-card suit is a major! With something like:

♠A Q ♡K 6 ◇J 8 7 4 ♣A Q 8 3 2

*with both long suits **minors**, and strength in **both** doubletons, 1NT is the best opening bid. You will have a major second-round bidding problem if you open 1♣ and partner responds 1♡ or 1♠.*

SOLUTION 95

♠ 7
♡ K J 6 4
♢ Q 8 7 3 2
♣ A Q 5

♠ A 6 2
♡ 9
♢ A K J 9 6 5
♣ 6 4 3

You open 1♢, partner responds 1♡, East overcalls 1♠, you try 2♢, and West jumps to 3♠, preemptive. Partner has heard enough and leaps to 5♢, the final bid. West leads a disconcerting ♣J. Plan the play (diamonds are 1-1).

You are looking at two possible club losers plus the ♡A. Even if West has underled the ♣K, there is no compelling reason to insert the ♣Q. If you take this trick with the ♣A, you can always take a second trick with the ♣Q later by leading up to it. The play of the ♣A prevents East from winning the ♣K and returning a club, setting up a second club winner before a heart winner can be established for a club discard. Given the bidding, it is surely correct, but the hand isn't over yet.

One plan is to win the ♣A, cross to a diamond and lead a heart to the ♡J. If this drives out the ♡A, the ♡K can be used to discard a club. Even if the ♡J loses to the ♡Q, you have enough dummy entries to trump two hearts hoping to flush out the ♡A. But there is even a better plan. Win the ♣A, strip the spades using the trump suit as communication, and then lead a heart to the ♡J. Say it loses to the ♡Q. Even if East has the expected ♡Q, any return presents you with the contract.

Notice West led his club sequence rather than his partner's suit. This may be West's last chance to be on lead. It is imaginative and often productive to lead from an honor sequence rather than partner's suit, particularly when one opponent may have a singleton in the suit that you and partner have been bidding madly. If the ♣J is not led, then the ♠K is the recommended lead; it may be important to hold the lead and make a killing shift if the ♠K wins the trick.

Tip:

It is an illusion to think you must always play the queen when dummy has AQx(x) and the suit is led. If you play the ace and later lead up to the queen, you still take a trick with the queen if the opening leader has the king.

The West hand: ♠K J 8 4 ♡8 7 5 3 ♢4 ♣J 10 9 2
The East hand: ♠Q 10 9 5 3 ♡A Q 10 2 ♢10 ♣K 8 7

SOLUTION 96

♠ A K 5 4 2
♡ 7 3
◇ J 6 5
♣ Q J 7

♠ J 9
♡ A Q
◇ A K 10 9 8
♣ K 4 3 2

You open 1◇, partner responds 1♠, East throws in a vulnerable 2♡ overcall, you try 2NT showing 17-18 HCP and partner bids 3NT. West leads the ♡2 to East's ♡K and your ♡A. Yes, a rank beginner can make this hand if East has the ◇Q but what if he doesn't? What if West has the ◇Q and returns a second heart? What then? Plan the play.

You definitely need a Plan B. If the diamond finesses loses and a heart comes back you won't have time to set up your ninth trick in clubs. However, if you attack clubs first and they break 3-3, you won't need the diamond finesse as you have nine tricks: three clubs and two tricks in each of the other three suits. So clubs before diamonds. But what if clubs are 4-2 and the diamond finesse doesn't work or are these thoughts too demoralizing?

There is a way out of this mess even if West has the ◇Q and even if clubs are 4-2. All you need is to find East with the ♣A, a card East figures to have on the bidding. Cross to a high spade at Trick 2 and lead a *low* club from dummy. Why?

Because if East rises with the ♣A to lead a heart you have three club tricks, or nine in all, only needing *two* diamond tricks.

If East plays low, win the ♣K and now play the ◇A, ◇K and another diamond, unblocking the ◇J from dummy. Nine tricks again: four diamonds, two hearts, two spades and one club. The key is leading a low club from dummy, not allowing East to capture an honor. This hand is similar to Problem 32. Remember?

The West hand: ♠Q 10 8 7 6 ♡8 4 2 ◇Q 4 3 ♣6 5
The East hand: ♠3 ♡K J 10 9 6 5 ◇7 2 ♣A 10 9 8

PROBLEM 97

♠ Q J 8
♡ 3
♢ 3 2
♣ A J 10 9 8 7 2

♠ A 10 9
♡ Q J 10 4 2
♢ A K 9 4
♣ K

Partner opens 3♣ and you opt for 3NT. West leads the ♠2, East plays the ♠3. Plan the play.

PROBLEM 98

♠ A 9 4 3
♡ J 6 4
♢ 7 3
♣ A 10 9 2

♠ Q J 10 8 6
♡ 10 8 3
♢ A K 2
♣ Q 4

You open fourth seat with 1♠, West doubles, partner bids a conventional 2NT (called 'Jordan') showing a limit raise in spades, a convention used only after a takeout double. With a natural 2NT bid, responder starts with a redouble. In any case, you sign off in 3♠, ending the bidding. West wastes no time cashing the ♡A, ♡K and ♡Q, East following up the line. At Trick 4 West shifts to the ♢J. Plan the play.

PROBLEM 99

♠ A Q 10 2
♡ 9 8
◇ Q 2
♣ J 10 4 3 2

♠ 4 3
♡ A 5 4
◇ K J 4 3
♣ A K Q 5

Your two little spades do not prevent you from opening 1NT. In fact, you have learned to put the ♣Q in with your spades to bolster your confidence. Partner responds 2♣, you bid 2◇ and partner bids 3NT. Sure enough they lead the ♠7, fourth best, but spades is partner's best suit! Plan the play.

PROBLEM 100 (*ADVANCED*)

♠ Q 4
♡ 8 6 4 3
◇ J 9 4
♣ K 4 3 2

♠ A 6
♡ A K 2
◇ A Q 10 3
♣ A J 10 5

You like your hand enough to open 2♣ and then rebid 2NT over partner's 2◇ response. Partner tries 3♣, you bid 3◇, and partner signs off in 3NT. West leads the ♠J. You try the ♠Q, but East is right there with the ♠K and you win the ♠A. Now what?

SOLUTION 97

♠ Q J 8
♡ 3
♢ 3 2
♣ A J 10 9 8 7 2

♠ A 10 9
♡ Q J 10 4 2
♢ A K 9 4
♣ K

Partner opens 3♣ and you opt for 3NT. West leads the ♠2, East plays the ♠3. Plan the play.

If your first two plays weren't black aces, you have misplayed the hand! The first black ace, the ♠A, is necessary to ensure a later spade entry to the club suit. The second black ace, the ♣A, is necessary both to unblock and to set up the suit, conceding a trick to the ♣Q, while a later spade entry to dummy still exists. You don't want to play the ♠A, the ♣K, and then enter dummy with a spade hoping the ♣Q drops. There would be no justice if it did.

Incidentally, you should play the ♠8 from dummy at Trick 1 to make certain you have a later spade entry to dummy just in case East has the ♠K and ducks.

This hand illustrates several points that come up time and time again:

Do not play too quickly to the first trick from either hand without looking over the entire hand and forming some plan.

Realize that when dummy has a powerful blocked suit you may have to create an extra dummy entry by winning a trick with a higher card than necessary. And let's not forget overtaking an honor with an honor to set up dummy's blocked suit while a dummy entry exists.

The West hand: ♠K 5 4 2 ♡7 6 5 ♢Q 8 6 5 ♣4 3
The East hand: ♠7 6 3 ♡A K 9 8 ♢J 10 7 ♣Q 6 5

If instead you bid 3♡ over 3♣, partner should bid 3♠ to show a spade *stopper*, not a spade suit. A 3♣ or 3♢ opening bid, in theory, denies a four-card major. The stopper-showing interpretation oftentimes allows the responder, the stronger hand, to bid 3NT after hearing about that stopper.

SOLUTION 98

♠ A 9 4 3
♡ J 6 4
♢ 7 3
♣ A 10 9 2

♠ Q J 10 8 6
♡ 10 8 3
♢ A K 2
♣ Q 4

You open fourth seat with 1♠, West doubles, partner bids a conventional 2NT (called 'Jordan') showing a limit raise in spades. In any case, you sign off in 3♠, ending the bidding. West wastes no time cashing the ♡A, ♡K and ♡Q, East following up the line. At Trick 4 West shifts to the ♢J. Plan the play.

It looks like the contract depends upon one of two black suit finesses working (75%). Unfortunately, you *know*, or should know, that neither is going to work! West, a passed hand, has already turned up with 10 HCP and can't realistically have either black king. What now?

On a good day East will have a singleton ♠K, but this may not be a good day. A better chance is to hope East has ♠Kx. Cross to the ♠A, leading the ♠Q in case West miscounted points or didn't see the ♠K the first time around. After taking the ♠A and no ♠K appearing, cash a second diamond and ruff a diamond, stripping that suit, and exit a spade. If East started with ♠Kx, East must either lead a club from his king or give you a ruff and sluff. If East leads a red card, ruff in dummy and discard a club from your hand. If East leads a club, go right up with the ♣Q. You know who has the ♣K.

When you know a finesse or more than one finesse can't possibly work, try to come up with something that might. Here a strip and throw-in is the answer.

The West hand: ♠7 5 ♡A K Q 7 ♢J 10 9 8 ♣J 8 7
The East hand: ♠K 2 ♡9 5 2 ♢Q 6 5 4 ♣K 6 5 3

Did you notice that the contract can be defeated if West shifts to a club at Trick 4? But how can West know? If you play that the lead of the queen can be made from the AKQ as well as from QJx, a playable convention and almost always readable, partner signals count under the queen and suit preference next. Here, East, holding the 952, plays the ♡2 at Trick 1 showing an odd number of hearts and then the ♡5, the lower of the two remaining hearts, suggesting a club shift. If East wanted a diamond shift, he would play the ♡2 then the ♡9. This lead convention is worth a try.

SOLUTION 99

♠ A Q 10 2
♡ 9 8
◇ Q 2
♣ J 10 4 3 2

♠ 4 3
♡ A 5 4
◇ K J 4 3
♣ A K Q 5

Your two little spades do not prevent you from opening 1NT. In fact, you have learned to put the ♣Q in with your spades to bolster your confidence. Partner responds 2♣, you bid 2◇ and partner bids 3NT. Sure enough they lead the ♠7, fourth best, but spades is partner's best suit! Plan the play.

Sometimes one (not you) can be so relieved by the sight of dummy that one (not you) may forget to count tricks! Assuming the ♠7 is a fourth best lead, some people (not you) don't bother applying the Rule of Eleven. This time the rule tells you that East has only one spade higher than the ♠7. If it is the ♠8 or ♠9, you can stick in the ♠10 and take three spade tricks. If it is the ♠8, ♠9 or ♠J, you can stick in the ♠Q and take two spade tricks. These are good bridge thoughts on other hands, but the real bridge thought should be the play of the spade suit in relation to *this* hand.

You simply cannot afford to let East in to switch to a heart before you have driven out the ◇A. Count your tricks! You have seven sure tricks with two more certain tricks in diamonds once the ace is driven out. You cannot go down if you win the first trick with the ♠A, run the clubs hoping for a diamond discard, and then attack diamonds starting with the ◇Q as you have the ♡A for a hand entry if they take the second diamond.

It is one thing to know how to handle a card combination in isolation, it is quite another to know how to handle the same combination in the context of the hand you are playing.

The West hand: ♠J 9 8 7 5 ♡K 7 6 3 ◇10 9 5 ♣9
The East hand: ♠K 6 ♡Q J 10 2 ◇A 8 7 6 ♣8 7 6

Playing matchpoints, you definitely have a Trick 1 problem as overtricks are so important. In fact, you should play the ♠Q, gambling that East's one spade higher than the ♠7 is not the ♠K. If the ♠Q holds, run your clubs before driving out the ◇A. If someone holding four diamonds discards one, you will take eleven tricks, otherwise ten.

SOLUTION 100 (*ADVANCED*)

♠ Q 4
♡ 8 6 4 3
◇ J 9 4
♣ K 4 3 2

♠ A 6
♡ A K 2
◇ A Q 10 3
♣ A J 10 5

You like your hand enough to open 2♣ and then rebid 2NT over partner's 2◇ response. Partner tries 3♣, you bid 3◇, and partner signs off in 3NT. West leads the ♠J. You try the ♠Q, but East is right there with the ♠K and you win the ♠A. Now what?

You have six top tricks plus two possible finesses on the horizon. If either loses you are a goner, so which one should you take? Normally you to try to combine chances by playing the ace-king of the suit missing the queen and if the queen doesn't appear, take a finesse in the suit missing the king. The trouble is that here even if the ♣Q does appear, you have only eight tricks and still need the diamond finesse. However, if the diamond finesse works, that's all you need as it gives you nine tricks: four diamonds, two hearts, at least two clubs and the ♠A.

It's not like anything terrible will happen if you play the ♣A and ♣K before attacking diamonds, but don't even think about taking a club finesse. It is a practice finesse if there ever was one. Even if it works, you still need the diamond finesse. And if it loses, don't ask.

But there's more. This diamond combination is tricky. Say you cross to the ♣K and run the ◇J and it holds. Now you lead a second diamond to your ten and that holds. But wait! The lead is in your hand and you can't return to dummy to repeat the finesse. East might have started with four or five diamonds. The best you can do is plunk down the ◇A, hoping the ◇K drops. If the ◇K doesn't drop, you have to bang down the ♣A and hope the ♣Q drops. Sort of pushing your luck.

But what if you start diamonds by leading the ◇9? East plays low, you underplay the ◇3, and after the ◇9 holds, lead the ◇J, underplaying the ◇10. You remain in dummy to repeat the finesse for a third time and take four diamond tricks no matter how many diamonds East has. Also start with the ◇9 holding ◇Q9x facing ◇AJ10x.

The West hand: ♠ J 10 9 8 3 ♡ 10 9 5 ◇ 8 7 ♣ Q 9 6
The East hand: ♠ K 7 5 2 ♡ Q J 7 ◇ K 6 5 2 ♣ 8 7

THE APPENDICES

APPENDIX 1: THE THEMES

These are the themes of the 100 hands:

1. Which of two finesses to take first. Staying alive.
2. Giving yourself an extra chance.
3. Counting tricks; playing safe; entry considerations; overtaking; IMPs vs. matchpoints.
4. Testing one suit before ducking a trick in another.
5. Staying alive with two finesse suits, one missing a queen, the other a jack. Spot cards.
6. How to handle two suits missing a queen where a winning finesse in either will give you the contract, but if you take the wrong one, down you go.
7. Trying to ruff out an honor in order to avoid taking a finesse. Using the bidding to place the missing honor cards.
8. Setting up a long suit to avoid a finesse in a shorter suit perhaps via an avoidance play.
9. Ducking a trick in a 4-3 fit to see if the suit breaks 3-3 before taking a possibly unneeded finesse.
10. Playing the odds when you are up against it.
11. Taking the 100% throw-in play rather than counting on one of three finesses to work.
12. Taking out insurance in case your main suit does not break evenly.
13. Best percentage play with two suits involved, one the trump suit.
14. Loser-on-loser play when setting up a long suit to avoid a possible dummy overruff.
15. Reading the lead and using a throw-in rather than taking a finesse.
16. Best percentage play when missing two kings.
17. Multiple finesse possibilities; avoidance finesse; card combinations.
18. Two finesses available; staying alive taking the right one first.
19. Combination play missing a king in one suit and a queen in the other.
20. Two finesses in long suits, one missing the queen, the other the king. What is the better chance?
21. Better percentage play – a finesse or a 3-3 break?
22. Combination plays and order of play.
23. Making the percentage discard.
24. Better percentage play: a 3-2 break in one suit or two finesses in another.
25. Combination play with two suits involved, one missing a queen, the other a king. Pay attention to the spot card led.
26. Ducking play at Trick 1 as an avoidance play.
27. Staying alive; trying to ruff out an honor in one suit before taking a finesse in another.

28. Preparing for a bad break in one suit with an alternative line of play.
29. Two-way suits; order of cashing winners; threat suits vs. non-threat suits. Counting the hand.
30. Trying to ruff out an honor in one suit before taking a finesse in another.
31. Long suit establishment before taking a finesse. Staying alive.
32. Counting tricks; sliding a low card past the player with the ace before taking a finesse in another suit.
33. Card combinations, entries; overtaking.
34. Better percentage play – a finesse or a 3-3 break?
35. Testing one suit so you will know what to do in another. Watch for defensive signaling.
36. Long-suit establishment before taking a finesse; staying alive.
37. Taking a needed finesse in a side suit to know how to play the trump suit.
38. Avoiding a finesse in an equal length suit via a loser-on-loser play; handling a ruff and a sluff properly.
39. Long-suit establishment vs. taking a finesse.
40. Notrump play strategy. Counting tricks. Which suit to attack?
41. Long-suit establishment before taking a finesse in another suit.
42. Long-suit establishment plus entry problems including a percentage play.
43. Counting tricks; Trick 1 play from dummy; card combinations.
44. Refusing a finesse; evening out the throw-in suit; strip and throw-in.
45. Percentage play; card combinations.
46. Avoiding a finesse via a loser-on-loser play when dummy has a void and declarer has the king.
47. When the bidding has marked the location of an important king. Card combinations; delaying a discard.
48. When 'eight ever, nine never' does not apply; trump suit management, avoidance finesse.
49. Strip and throw-in plus an avoidance play at Trick 1 to keep the danger hand off lead.
50. When two queens are missing what is the best percentage play?
51. Evening out a side suit in preparation for a strip and throw-in.
52. Dummy reversal technique; entry considerations.
53. Two equally-divided suits each missing a queen for one loser. Strip and endplay technique.
54. Card combinations; percentage play involving two suits.
55. Card combinations. The *finesse obbligato*.
56. Two suits each missing a king; ruffing out an honor to avoid a finesse in a short suit.
57. Combining chances in three suits.
58. Avoidance hold-up play and an avoidance trump finesse into the non-danger hand.

59. Example of an avoidance ruffing finesse.
60. Two chances are better than one; staying alive.
61. Counting tricks. Finessing into the non-danger hand. Looking ahead. Entry considerations.
62. Avoidance finesse; matchpoint strategy vs. IMP strategy.
63. When to hold up. Counting the opponents' points to place the missing honors. Matchpoint strategy.
64. Ruffing finesse vs. straight finesse.
65. Throw-in play rather than taking a finesse.
66. Extra chances by delaying a discard.
67. Card combinations; ducking play; entry considerations.
68. When not to hold up; order of cashing tricks; card combinations. Allowing for a blocked suit.
69. Avoidance finesse to prevent a possibly damaging lead through an unprotected honor.
70. Using an equal-length side suit as the throw-in suit to avoid a guess in a side suit.
71. Having enough entries to reverse dummy for an extra trick.
72. Counting trump tricks on a crossruff hand to determine whether you need to risk a finesse.
73. Planning the play at Trick 1; blocked suits; entry considerations.
74. A throw-in play to force the player who is thrown in to give you a trick in return.
75. Which finesse? An exception to the rule. Entry considerations.
76. Card combinations; minimum number of tricks needed in your best suit.
77. Counting tricks; entries; when not to finesse; looking ahead.
78. Counting sure tricks; matchpoint strategy vs. IMP strategy.
79. Using the trump suit as the throw-in suit rather than taking a finesse; card combinations.
80. Practice finesses; taking one finesse rather than two.
81. Getting rid of an eventual loser by disdaining a finesse. Time considerations. Looking ahead; card combinations.
82. Loser-on-loser play when dummy has a void in the suit that has been led and the opponents have the ace and king. Gaining a trick by discarding a slow loser.
83. Placing the cards. Throw-in rather than taking a finesse that is sure to lose.
84. Trying to set up an honor card via trumping before taking a finesse. Two chances are better than one.
85. Long-suit establishment; entries; two chances; card combinations. Unblocking in preparation for a possible later finesse.
86. Percentage play; deciding between a finesse and a 3-3 break.

87. Two suits to work with; trying to ruff out a missing a queen before taking a finesse for a missing king.
88. Playing the odds. Length attracts shortness; shortness attracts length.
89. A practice finesse; card combinations; stripping the hand with losers in one suit that has to be attacked by declarer; the Crocodile Coup.
90. Two blocked suits; entries; winning the race to discard a slow loser.
91. Desperation vs. safety depending upon how trumps break.
92. Using the bidding to locate an important honor; the backwards finesse.
93. Long-suit establishment; the ducking play to retain control of a suit; entry considerations; ruffing losers.
94. Which suit to establish? Playing with the odds.
95. Card combinations; strip and throw-in; imaginative opening lead possibilities with a weak hand.
96. Sliding a low card past the player with the ace, giving that player a Hobson's Choice: damned if you do, damned if you don't.
97. Playing to the first trick; overtaking an honor with an honor; entry considerations.
98. When an opponent has passed originally; placing the cards; trump throw-in.
99. Counting your sure tricks; Rule of Eleven; IMP strategy vs. matchpoint strategy.
100. Card combinations. Counting needed tricks.

APPENDIX 2: USEFUL NUMBERS

Here are some helpful numbers to keep in mind (*note that these are all rounded off to avoid decimals*).

When you have seven cards between your hand and dummy:

- The suit is likely to be divided 3-3 36% of the time.
- The suit is likely to be divided 4-2 48% of the time. (If you can make your contract if a suit is divided either 3-3 or 4-2, you have an 84% chance of making your contract)
- If you are missing an honor, that honor is apt to be singleton 3% and doubleton 16% of the time.

When you have eight cards between your hand and dummy:

- The suit is likely to be divided 3-2 68% of the time.
- The suit is likely to be divided 4-1 28% of the time.
- If you are missing an honor, that honor is apt to be singleton 6% and doubleton 27% of the time.

When you have nine cards between your hand and dummy:

- The suit is likely to be divided 2-2 40% of the time.
- The suit is likely to be divided 3-1 50% of the time.
- If you are missing an honor, that honor is likely to be singleton 12% and doubleton 40% of the time.

When you have ten cards in a suit missing the king, finesse for the king (50%). If you play the ace hoping to drop the singleton king, you will be right only 26% of the time.

When you have eleven cards in a suit missing the king, play for the drop (52%).

Combination percentages.

- If a contract depends upon one finesse, you have a 50% chance of making your contract.
- If a contract depends upon making one of two finesses, you have a 75% chance of making your contract.
- If a contract depends upon making both of two finesses, you have a 25% chance of making your contract.
- If a contract depends upon a finesse or a 3-3 division in another suit, you have a 68% chance of making your contract.
- If a contract depends upon a finesse or a 3-2 break in another suit, you have an 84% chance of making your contract.

When you need two good things to happen (cross your fingers)

- If a contract depends upon two suits each breaking 3-3, you have a 13% chance of making your contract.
- If a contract depends upon a finesse plus a 3-3 break in another suit, you have an 18% chance of making your contract.
- If a contract depends upon a finesse plus a 3-2 break in another suit, you have a 34% chance of making your contract.

Go get 'em!

MASTER POINT PRESS ON THE INTERNET

WWW.MASTERPOINTPRESS.COM

Our main site, with information about our books and software, reviews and more.

WWW.MASTERINGBRIDGE.COM

Our site for bridge teachers and students — free downloadable support material for our books, helpful articles, forums and more.

WWW.BRIDGEBLOGGING.COM

Read and comment on regular articles from MPP authors and other bridge notables.

WWW.EBOOKSBRIDGE.COM

Purchase downloadable electronic versions of MPP books and software.